THE BIG BOOK OF LITTLE Amigurumi

THE BIG BOOK OF LITTLE Amigurumi

72 Seriously Cute Patterns to Crochet

Ana Paula Rímoli

Martingale®
Create with Confidence

The Big Book of Little Amigurumi:
72 Seriously Cute Patterns to Crochet
© 2014 by Ana Paula Rímoli

Martingale®
19021 120th Ave. NE, Ste. 102
Bothell, WA 98011-9511 USA
ShopMartingale.com

Printed in China
19 18 17 16 15 14   8 7 6 5 4 3 2 1

**Library of Congress Cataloging-in-Publication Data
is available upon request.**

ISBN: 978-1-60468-581-7

Mission Statement

Dedicated to providing quality products
and service to inspire creativity.

Credits

PRESIDENT AND CHIEF VISIONARY OFFICER:
Jennifer Erbe Keltner

EDITOR IN CHIEF: Mary V. Green

DESIGN DIRECTOR: Paula Schlosser

MANAGING EDITOR: Karen Costello Soltys

ACQUISITIONS EDITOR: Karen M. Burns

PRODUCTION MANAGER: Regina Girard

COVER AND INTERIOR DESIGNER: Paula Schlosser

COMPOSITION AND LAYOUT: Dianna Logan, DBS

PHOTOGRAPHER: Brent Kane

ILLUSTRATOR: Laurel Strand

Dedication

Para Oli y Marti, las quiero hasta el cielo!

Contents

Introduction

Welcome to my great big book of amigurumi!
I'm so excited to have so many of my patterns in one book.

I learned to crochet when I was seven years old and I've been stitching ever since. When my daughters, Oli and Martina, were born, I no longer had the time or patience for long, elaborate projects, so I started making little toys for them instead. That's when I discovered amigurumi, and I was hooked.

Oli and Martina are now 11 and 7 years old, and I'm still making amigurumi. I can't help myself! They are so fast and fun to make. Most of the "amis" (as they're affectionately called) in the book can be finished in a couple of hours and make great gifts for kids and grown-ups alike (lots of people are now collecting them). Amigurumi are crocheted in the round, mainly using a single crochet stitch, so they're very easy to make.

This book includes some of my favorite toys. Some are in sets, like the tea set and the mama turtle with her eggs, and others are just single, like the sweet unicorn. All of them will invite imaginative, creative play.

I hope you'll find making these little characters as addictive and fun as I have.

Ana

Valentine Bears

Everybody needs a little teddy bear (or two). Valentino and Valentina are the perfect size; they are super fast to make and the sweetest little pair to give as a present.

Finished Sizes

Girl and boy bears: Approx 5½" tall

Materials

Worsted-weight yarn in brown, pink, red, and white

Size G-6 (4 mm) crochet hook

9 mm plastic eyes with safety backings

Small piece of tan craft felt

Sewing thread and sharp needle

Black embroidery floss and tapestry needle

Fiberfill or stuffing of your choice

Small beads or buttons for earrings

Girl or Boy Bear

Head

Rnd 1: Using brown yarn, ch 2, 6 sc in second chain from hook.

Rnd 2: Sc 2 in each sc around. (12 sts)

Rnd 3: *Sc 1, 2 sc in next sc*, rep 6 times. (18 sts)

Rnd 4: *Sc 2, 2 sc in next sc*, rep 6 times. (24 sts)

Rnd 5: *Sc 3, 2 sc in next sc*, rep 6 times. (30 sts)

Rnds 6–13: Sc 30.

Rnd 14: *Sc 3, dec 1*, rep 6 times. (24 sts)

Rnd 15: *Sc 2, dec 1*, rep 6 times. (18 sts)

Attach eyes. Cut muzzle from felt using pattern on page 12 and embroider nose and mouth. Sew muzzle to head.

Rnd 16: Sc 18.

Stuff almost to top.

Rnd 17: *Sc 1, dec 1*, rep 6 times. (12 sts)

Finish stuffing.

Fasten off and weave in loose ends.

Ears

Make 2.

Rnd 1: Using brown yarn, ch 2, 6 sc in second chain from hook.

Rnd 2: Sc 2 in each sc around. (12 sts)

Rnds 3 and 4: Sc 12.

Fasten off, leaving a long tail for sewing, and sew to head.

Sew little buttons or beads to Valentina's ears for earrings.

Body

Start with red yarn if making Valentino or white yarn (underwear) if making Valentina.

Rnd 1: Ch 2, 6 sc in second chain from hook.

Rnd 2: 2 sc in each sc around. (12 sts)

Rnd 3: *Sc 1, 2 sc in next sc*, rep 6 times. (18 sts)

Rnd 4: *Sc 2, 2 sc in next sc*, rep 6 times. (24 sts)

Rnds 5–8: Sc 24.

For girl:

Rnd 9: Change to skirt color, sc 24.

Rnd 10: Sc 24 through back loops only (you'll use the front loops later when crocheting the skirt).

Rnd 11: Sc 24.

For boy:

Rnds 9–11: Sc 24.

For both:

Rnd 12: *Sc 2, dec 1*, rep 6 times. (18 sts)

Rnd 13: Sc 18.

Fasten off, leaving a long tail for sewing. Stuff and sew to head.

Arms and Legs

Make 2 of each.

Rnd 1: Using brown yarn, ch 2, 8 sc in second chain from hook.

Rnd 2: Sc 8.

For arms:

Rep rnd 2 another 7 times. Fasten off, leaving a long tail for sewing. Stuff, sew open end closed, and sew to body.

For legs:

Rep rnd 2 another 5 times. Fasten off, leaving a long tail for sewing. Stuff and sew to body.

Skirt for Girl

Holding bear upside down (legs up in the air), join pink yarn at back of body to one of the front loops you left in rnd 10 of the body.

Rnd 1: Sc 24 through front loops all around the body.

Rnd 2: 2 sc in each sc around. (48 sts)

Rnd 3: Sc 48.

Rep rnd 3 until you're happy with the skirt length. Fasten off and weave in ends.

Scarf for Boy

Using pink yarn, loosely ch 40, turn.

Ch 2, hdc in third ch from hook and in each ch across.

Fasten off and weave in ends.

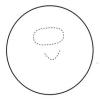

Bear muzzle

Baby Lion and His Daddy

When I was little, my cousins and I used to go to a small zoo in the countryside where a single lion was kept in the saddest cage. He would stand on his hind legs, jump on the bars, roar, and scare us silly. I still think about him once in a while, and I just had to make him a friend and imagine him all happiness and smiles.

Finished Sizes

Daddy: Approx 7½" tall
Baby: Approx 4" tall

Materials

Worsted-weight yarn in gold and orange
Size G-6 (4 mm) and E-4 (3.5 mm) crochet hooks
6 mm and 9 mm plastic eyes with safety backings
Small piece of tan craft felt

Sewing thread and sharp needle
Brown embroidery floss and tapestry needle
Fiberfill or stuffing of your choice

Daddy Lion

Use gold yarn for everything except the mane and the tip of the tail.

Head

Rnd 1: Using G hook, ch 2, 6 sc in second ch from hook.
Rnd 2: Sc 2 in each sc around. (12 sts)
Rnd 3: *Sc 1, 2 sc in next sc*, rep 6 times. (18 sts)
Rnd 4: *Sc 2, 2 sc in next sc*, rep 6 times. (24 sts)
Rnd 5: *Sc 3, 2 sc in next sc*, rep 6 times. (30 sts)
Rnd 6: *Sc 4, 2 sc in next sc*, rep 6 times. (36 sts)
Rnd 7: *Sc 5, 2 sc in next sc*, rep 6 times. (42 sts)
Rnds 8–19: Sc 42.
Rnd 20: *Sc 5, dec 1*, rep 6 times. (36 sts)

Rnd 21: *Sc 4, dec 1*, rep 6 times. (30 sts)
Attach eyes. Cut muzzle from felt, embroider nose and mouth, and sew muzzle to head.
Rnd 22: *Sc 3, dec 1*, rep 6 times. (24 sts)
Rnd 23: *Sc 2, dec 1*, rep 6 times. (18 sts)
Rnd 24: *Sc 1, dec 1*, rep 6 times. (12 sts)
Stuff head.
Rnd 25: *Sk 1 sc, sc 1*, rep 6 times. (6 sts)
Fasten off and weave in ends.

Mane

Using G hook and orange yarn, loosely ch 45.
4 tr in fourth ch from hook, sk 1 sc, sl st 1, *5 tr in next st, sk 1 sc, sl st 1, rep from * 13 times.
Fasten off, leaving a long tail for sewing. Sew both ends tog and place mane on lion's head as if it were a headband. When you're happy with the position of the mane, sew it in place.

Ears

Make 2.

Rnd 1: Using G hook, ch 2, 5 sc in second ch from hook.

Rnd 2: Sc 2 in each sc around. (10 sts)

Rnd 3: Sc 10.

Fasten off, leaving a long tail for sewing, and sew to head in front of mane.

Body

Rnd 1: Using G hook, ch 2, 6 sc in second ch from hook.

Rnd 2: Sc 2 in each sc around. (12 sts)

Rnd 3: *Sc 1, 2 sc in next sc*, rep 6 times. (18 sts)

Rnd 4: *Sc 2, 2 sc in next sc*, rep 6 times. (24 sts)

Rnds 5–14: Sc 24.

Rnd 15: *Sc 2, dec 1*, rep 6 times. (18 sts)

Rnds 16 and 17: Sc 18.

Fasten off, leaving a long tail for sewing. Stuff and sew to head.

Legs and Arms

Make 2 of each.

Rnd 1: Using G hook, ch 2, 5 sc in second ch from hook.

Rnd 2: Sc 2 in each sc around. (10 sts)

Arms:

Rnds 3–15: Sc 10.

Fasten off, leaving a long tail for sewing. Stuff, sew open end closed, and sew arm to body.

Legs:

Rnds 3–12: Sc 10.

Fasten off, leaving a long tail for sewing. Stuff, sew open end closed, and sew leg to body.

Tail

Rnd 1: Using G hook and orange yarn, ch 2, 6 sc in second ch from hook.

Rnd 2: Sc 6.

Rnd 3: Sc 2 in each sc around. (12 sts)

Rnd 4: *Sk 1 sc, sc 1*, rep 6 times. (6 sts)

Stuff end a little and change to gold yarn.

Rnd 5: Sc 6.

Rep rnd 5 until tail is approx 3½" long.

Fasten off, leaving a long tail for sewing, and sew to body.

Baby

Use gold yarn for everything except the mane.

Head

Rnd 1: Using E hook, ch 2, 6 sc in second ch from hook.

Rnd 2: Sc 2 in each sc around. (12 sts)

Rnd 3: *Sc 1, 2 sc in next sc*, rep 6 times. (18 sts)

Rnd 4: *Sc 2, 2 sc in next sc*, rep 6 times. (24 sts)

Rnd 5: *Sc 3, 2 sc in next sc*, rep 6 times. (30 sts)

Rnds 6–14: Sc 30.

Attach eyes. Cut muzzle from felt using pattern on page 16 and embroider nose and mouth. Sew muzzle to head.

Rnd 15: *Sc 3, dec 1*, rep 6 times.
(24 sts)

Rnd 16: *Sc 2, dec 1*, rep 6 times.
(18 sts)

Rnd 17: *Sc 1, dec 1*, rep 6 times.
(12 sts)

Stuff head.

Rnd 18: *Sk 1 sc, sc 1*, rep 6 times.
(6 sts)

Fasten off and weave in ends.

Mane

Using E hook, loosely ch 38 sts.

4 hdc in third ch from hook, sk 1 sc,
sl st 1, *5 hdc in next st, sk 1 sc,
sl st 1*, rep from * to * 11 times.

Fasten off, leaving a long tail for sewing.
Join ends and place mane on lion's
head as if it were a headband. When
you're happy with the position of the
mane, sew it in place.

Body

Rnd 1: Using E hook, ch 2, 6 sc in
second ch from hook.

Rnd 2: Sc 2 in each sc around. (12 sts)

Rnd 3: *Sc 1, 2 sc in next sc*, rep
6 times. (18 sts)

Rnds 4–8: Sc 18.

Rnd 9: *Sc 1, dec 1*, rep 6 times. (12 sts)

Fasten off, leaving a long tail for sewing.
Stuff and sew to head.

Legs and Arms

Make 4.

Rnd 1: Using E hook, ch 2, 6 sc in
second ch from hook.

Rnds 2–5: Sc 6.

Fasten off, leaving a long tail for sewing.
Lightly stuff arms, sew open end
closed, and sew to body. Lightly stuff
legs and sew to body.

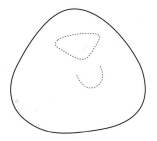

Daddy lion muzzle

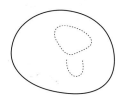

Baby lion muzzle

Puppy and His Daddy

Talk about convenient—these dogs are already housebroken, they won't bark at strangers, and they make great cuddle friends! Did I mention they're also super quick to crochet?

Finished Sizes

Daddy: Approx 7" long
Puppy: Approx 4½" tall

Materials

Worsted-weight yarn in black, orange, and brown
Size G-6 (4.5 mm) crochet hook
9 mm plastic eyes with safety backings
Black embroidery floss and tapestry needle
Fiberfill or stuffing of your choice

Daddy

Nose

Rnd 1: Using black yarn, ch 2, 8 sc in second ch from hook.
Rnd 2: Sc 2 in each sc around. (16 sts)
Fasten off, leaving a long tail for sewing, and set aside.

Eye Spot

Rnd 1: Using brown yarn, ch 2, 6 sc in second ch from hook.
Rnd 2: Sc 2 in each sc around. (12 sts)
Rnd 3: Sc 5, 4 sc in next sc, sc 6.
Fasten off, leaving a long tail for sewing, and set aside.

Head

The head is started from the nose end.
Rnd 1: Using orange yarn, ch 2, 6 sc in second ch from hook.
Rnd 2: Sc 2 in each sc around. (12 sts)
Rnd 3: *Sc 1, 2 sc in next sc*, rep 6 times. (18 sts)
Rnd 4: *Sc 2, 2 sc in next sc*, rep 6 times. (24 sts)
Rnd 5: *Sc 3, 2 sc in next sc*, rep 6 times. (30 sts)
Rnd 6: *Sc 4, 2 sc in next sc*, rep 6 times. (36 sts)

Rnds 7–16: Sc 36.
Rnd 17: *Sc 4, dec 1*, rep 6 times. (30 sts)
Sew nose to head.
Rnds 18 and 19: Sc 30.
Rnd 20: *Sc 3, dec 1*, rep 6 times. (24 sts)
Rnds 21–23: Sc 24.
Insert one eye into center of the eye spot, attach eye to head, and sew spot to head.
Attach second eye to head. Embroider mouth.

Rnd 24: *Sc 2, dec 1*, rep 6 times. (18 sts)

Stuff head almost to top.

Rnd 25: *Sc 1, dec 1*, rep 6 times. (12 sts)

Finish stuffing.

Rnd 26: *Sk 1 sc, sc 1*, rep 6 times. (6 sts)

Fasten off and weave in ends.

Ears

Make 2.

Rnd 1: Using brown yarn, ch 2, 5 sc in second ch from hook.

Rnd 2: Sc 2 in each sc around. (10 sts)

Rnds 3–11: Sc 10.

Fasten off, leaving a long tail for sewing. Stuff and sew to head.

Body

Rnd 1: Using orange yarn, ch 2, 6 sc in second ch from hook.

Rnd 2: Sc 2 in each sc around. (12 sts)

Rnd 3: *Sc 1, 2 sc in next sc*, rep 6 times. (18 sts)

Rnd 4: *Sc 2, 2 sc in next sc*, rep 6 times. (24 sts)

Rnd 5: *Sc 3, 2 sc in next sc*, rep 6 times. (30 sts)

Rnds 6–15: Sc 30.

Rnd 16: *Sc 3, dec 1*, rep 6 times. (24 sts)

Rnd 17: Sc 24.

Rnd 18: *Sc 2, dec 1*, rep 6 times. (18 sts)

Rnds 19–21: Sc 18.

Fasten off, leaving a long tail for sewing. Stuff and sew to head.

Legs

Make 4.

Rnd 1: Using orange yarn, ch 2, 5 sc in second ch from hook.

Rnd 2: Sc 2 in each sc around. (10 sts)

Rnds 3–9: Sc 10.

Fasten off, leaving a long tail for sewing. Stuff and sew to body.

To make a leg with a different color foot, work rnds 1–4 with contrast color, then work the rem rnds with body color.

Tail

Rnd 1: Using brown yarn, ch 2, 5 sc in second ch from hook.

Rnds 2–4: Sc 5.

Fasten off, leaving a long tail for sewing, and sew to body. No need to stuff the tail.

Puppy

Nose

Rnd 1: Using black yarn, ch 2, 5 sc in second ch from hook.

Rnd 2: Sc 2 in each sc around. (10 sts)

Fasten off, leaving a long tail for sewing, and set aside.

Eye Spot

Rnd 1: Using orange yarn, ch 2, 5 sc in second ch from hook.

Rnd 2: Sc 2 in each sc around. (10 sts)

Fasten off, leaving a long tail for sewing, and set aside.

Head

Rnd 1: Using brown yarn, ch 2, 5 sc in second ch from hook.

Rnd 2: Sc 2 in each sc around. (10 sts)

Rnd 3: *Sc 1, 2 sc in next sc*, rep 5 times. (15 sts)

Body

Rnd 1: Using brown yarn, ch 2, 5 sc in second ch from hook.

Rnd 2: Sc 2 in each sc around. (10 sts)

Rnd 3: *Sc 1, 2 sc in next sc*, rep 5 times. (15 sts)

Rnd 4: *Sc 2, 2 sc in next sc*, rep 5 times. (20 sts)

Rnds 5–8: Sc 20.

Rnd 9: *Sc 2, dec 1*, rep 5 times. (15 sts)

Rnds 10–13: Sc 15.

Fasten off, leaving a long tail for sewing. Stuff and sew to head.

Legs

Make 4.

Rnd 1: Using brown yarn, ch 2, 4 sc in second ch from hook.

Rnd 2: Sc 2 in each sc around. (8 sts)

Rnds 3–6: Sc 8.

Fasten off, leaving a long tail for sewing. Stuff and sew to body.

Make 1 leg in contrast color if desired.

Tail

Rnd 1: Using orange yarn, ch 2, 4 sc in second ch from hook.

Rnds 2 and 3: Sc 4.

Fasten off, leaving a long tail for sewing, and sew to body. No need to stuff tail.

Rnd 4: *Sc 2, 2 sc in next sc*, rep 5 times. (20 sts)

Rnd 5: *Sc 3, 2 sc in next sc*, rep 5 times. (25 sts)

Rnd 6–13: Sc 25.

Insert one eye into center of eye spot, attach eye to head, and sew spot to head.

Attach second eye to head. Sew nose on head.

Rnd 14: *Sc 3, dec 1*, rep 5 times. (20 sts)

Rnds 15–17: Sc 20.

Rnd 18: *Sc 2, dec 1*, rep 5 times. (15 sts)

Stuff head almost to top.

Rnd 19: *Sc 1, dec 1*, rep 5 times. (10 sts)

Finish stuffing.

Rnd 20: *Sk 1 sc, sc 1*, rep 5 times. (5 sts)

Fasten off and weave in ends.

Ears

Make 2.

Rnd 1: Using brown yarn, ch 2, 4 sc in second ch from hook.

Rnd 2: Sc 2 in each sc around. (8 sts)

Rnds 3–7: Sc 8.

Fasten off, leaving a long tail for sewing. Stuff and sew to head.

Baby Monkey and Her Daddy

Who doesn't love monkeys? They're fun, playful, and cute—and lots of fun to crochet, too. Make Daddy and Baby Monkey, and *your* little monkeys will jump around in joy. To make Mommy monkey, add a skirt and earrings to the Daddy pattern.

Finished Sizes

Daddy: Approx 10" tall
Baby: Approx 6" tall

Materials

Worsted-weight yarn in brown and red
Size G-6 (4 mm) crochet hook
9 mm plastic eyes with safety backings
Small piece of tan craft felt
Sewing thread and sharp needle
Brown embroidery floss and tapestry needle
Fiberfill or stuffing of your choice
2 little buttons or beads for earrings (4 buttons if making Mommy)

Daddy

Head

Rnd 1: Using brown yarn, ch 2, 6 sc in second ch from hook.
Rnd 2: Sc 2 in each sc around. (12 sts)
Rnd 3: *Sc 1, 2 sc in next sc*, rep 6 times. (18 sts)
Rnd 4: *Sc 2, 2 sc in next sc*, rep 6 times. (24 sts)
Rnd 5: *Sc 3, 2 sc in next sc*, rep 6 times. (30 sts)
Rnd 6: *Sc 4, 2 sc in next sc*, rep 6 times. (36 sts)
Rnd 7: *Sc 5, 2 sc in next sc*, rep 6 times. (42 sts)
Rnds 8–19: Sc 42.
Rnd 20: *Sc 5, dec 1*, rep 6 times. (36 sts)
Rnd 21: *Sc 4, dec 1*, rep 6 times. (30 sts)
Cut out muzzle and eye pieces from felt. Embroider nose and mouth on muzzle and sew to head. Cut a little slit in middle of eye pieces, insert eyes through slits, and secure to head. Sew felt pieces to head.
Rnd 22: Sc 30.
Rnd 23: *Sc 3, dec 1*, rep 6 times. (24 sts)
Rnd 24: *Sc 2, dec 1*, rep 6 times. (18 sts)
Rnd 25: *Sc 1, dec 1*, rep 6 times. (12 sts)
Stuff head.
Rnd 26: *Sk 1 sc, sc 1*, rep 6 times. (6 sts)
Fasten off and weave in ends.

Ears

Make 2.
Rnd 1: Using brown yarn, ch 2, 6 sc in second ch from hook.
Rnd 2: Sc 2 in each sc around. (12 sts)
Rnds 3–5: Sc 12.
Fasten off, leaving a long tail for sewing, and sew to head.

Body

Rnd 1: Using brown yarn, ch 2, 6 sc in second ch from hook.
Rnd 2: Sc 2 in each sc around. (12 sts)
Rnd 3: *Sc 1, 2 sc in next sc*, rep 6 times. (18 sts)
Rnd 4: *Sc 2, 2 sc in next sc*, rep 6 times. (24 sts)
Rnd 5: *Sc 3, 2 sc in next sc*, rep 6 times. (30 sts)
Rnds 6–11: Sc 30.

Legs

Make 2.

Rnd 1: Using brown yarn, ch 2, 6 sc in second ch from hook.

Rnd 2: Sc 2 in each sc around. (12 sts)

Rnds 3–17: Sc 12, stuffing as you go.

Fasten off, leaving a long tail for sewing, and sew to body.

Tail

Rnd 1: Using brown yarn, ch 2, 8 sc in second ch from hook.

Rnd 2: Sc 8.

Rep rnd 2, stuffing as you go, until tail is approx 6" long.

Fasten off, leaving a long tail for sewing, and sew to body.

For Daddy:

Rnd 12: Change to red yarn, sc 30.

Rnd 13: BPsc 30.

For Mommy:

Rnd 12: Change to red yarn, sc 30 through back loops only (you'll use the front loops later when crocheting the skirt).

Rnd 13: Sc 30.

For both:

Rnds 14–20: Sc 30.

Rnd 21: *Sc 3, dec 1*, rep 6 times. (24 sts)

Rnd 22: Sc 24.

Rnd 23: *Sc 2, dec 1*, rep 6 times. (18 sts)

Rnd 24: Sc 18.

Stuff body.

Fasten off, leaving a long tail for sewing, and sew to head.

Arms

Make 2.

Rnd 1: Using brown yarn, ch 2, 6 sc in second ch from hook.

Rnd 2: Sc 2 in each sc around. (12 sts)

Rnds 3–23: Sc 12, stuffing as you go.

Rnd 24: Change to red yarn, sc 12.

Rnd 25: BPsc 12.

Rnds 26–35: Sc 12, stuffing as you go.

Fasten off, leaving a long tail for sewing. Sew open end closed and sew to body.

Skirt for Mommy (optional)

Holding doll upside down (legs up in the air), join red yarn at back of body to 1 of the front loops you left in rnd 12 when making body.

Rnd 1: Sc 30 through front loops all around body.

Rnd 2: Sc 2 in each sc around. (60 sts)

Rnd 3: Sc 60.

Rep rnd 3 until you're happy with the skirt length.

Fasten off and weave in ends.

Baby

Head

Rnd 1: Using brown yarn, ch 2, 6 sc in second ch from hook.

Rnd 2: Sc 2 in each sc around. (12 sts)

Rnd 3: *Sc 1, 2 sc in next sc*, rep 6 times. (18 sts)

Rnd 4: *Sc 2, 2 sc in next sc*, rep 6 times. (24 sts)

Rnd 5: *Sc 3, 2 sc in next sc*, rep 6 times. (30 sts)

Rnds 6–14: Sc 30.

Cut out muzzle and eye pieces from felt using pattern on page 25. Embroider nose and mouth on muzzle and sew to head. Cut a little slit in middle of eye pieces, insert eyes through slits, and secure to head. Sew felt pieces to head.

Rnd 15: *Sc 3, dec 1*, rep 6 times. (24 sts)

Rnd 16: Sc 24.

Rnd 17: *Sc 2, dec 1*, rep 6 times. (18 sts)

Rnd 18: *Sc 1, dec 1*, rep 6 times. (12 sts)

Stuff head.

Rnd 19: *Sk 1 sc, sc 1*, rep 6 times. (6 sts)

Fasten off and weave in ends.

Ears

Make 2.

Rnd 1: Using brown yarn, ch 2, 5 sc in second ch from hook.

Rnd 2: Sc 2 in each sc around. (10 sts)

Rnds 3 and 4: Sc 10.

Fasten off, leaving a long tail for sewing. Sew little buttons or beads to ear lobes and sew ears to head.

Body

Rnd 1: Using brown yarn, ch 2, 6 sc in second ch from hook.

Rnd 2: Sc 2 in each sc around. (12 sts)

Rnd 3: *Sc 1, 2 sc in next sc*, rep 6 times. (18 sts)

Rnd 4: *Sc 2, 2 sc in next sc*, rep 6 times. (24 sts)

Rnds 5 and 6: Sc 24.

For girl:

Rnd 7: Change to red yarn, sc 24 through back loops only (you'll use the front loops later when crocheting the skirt)

Rnd 8: Sc 24.

For boy:

Rnd 7: Change to red yarn, sc 24.

Rnd 8: BPsc 24.

For both:

Rnds 9–11: Sc 24.

Rnd 12: *Sc 2, dec 1*, rep 6 times. (18 sts)

Rnd 13: Sc 18.

Stuff body.

Fasten off, leaving a long tail for sewing, and sew to head.

Arms

Make 2.

Rnd 1: Using brown yarn, ch 2, 4 sc in second ch from hook.

Rnd 2: 2 Sc 2 in each sc around. (8 sts)

Rnds 3–7: Sc 8, stuffing as you go.

Rnd 8: Change to red yarn, sc 8.

Rnd 9: BPsc 8.

Rnds 10–19: Sc 8, stuffing as you go.

Fasten off, leaving a long tail for sewing. Sew open end closed and sew to body.

Legs

Make 2.

Rnd 1: Using brown yarn, ch 2, 4 sc in second ch from hook.

Rnd 2: Sc 2 in each sc around. (8 sts)

Rnds 3–9: Sc 8, stuffing as you go.

Fasten off, leaving a long tail for sewing, and sew to body.

Tail

Rnd 1: Using brown yarn, ch 2, 5 sc in second ch from hook.

Rnd 2: Sc 5.

Rep rnd 2, stuffing as you go, until tail is approx 2½" long.

Fasten off, leaving a long tail for sewing, and sew to body.

Skirt

Holding doll upside down (legs up in the air), join red yarn at back of body to one of front loops you left in rnd 7 when making body.

Rnd 1: Sc 24 through front loops all around body.

Rnd 2: Sc 2 in each sc around. (48 sts)

Rnd 3: Sc 48.

Rep rnd 3 until you're happy with the skirt length. Fasten off and weave in ends.

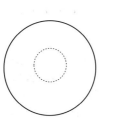

Monkey eye

Daddy monkey muzzle

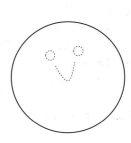

Baby monkey muzzle

Baby Penguin and Her Mommy

After watching March of the Penguins and Happy Feet, my daughter Oli wouldn't stop talking about penguins and walking like a little penguin, so I had to make some.

Finished Sizes

Mommy: Approx 6½" tall
Baby: Approx 4½" tall

Materials

Worsted-weight yarn in black, blue, yellow, and white
Size G-6 (4 mm) and F-5 (3.75 mm) crochet hooks
9 mm plastic eyes with safety backings
Fiberfill or stuffing of your choice

Mommy

Eye Roundies

Make 2.
Rnd 1: Using F hook and blue yarn, ch 2, 6 sc in second ch from hook.
Rnd 2: Sc 2 in each sc around. (12 sts)
Rnd 3: *Sc 1, 2 sc in next sc*, rep 6 times. (18 sts)
Fasten off, leaving a long tail for sewing, and set aside.

Beak

Rnd 1: Using F hook and yellow yarn, ch 2, 5 sc in second ch from hook.
Rnd 2: Sc 2 in each sc around. (10 sts)
Rnd 3: Sc 10.

Rnd 4: *Sc 1, 2 sc in next sc*, rep 5 times. (15 sts)
Rnds 5 and 6: Sc 15.
Fasten off, leaving a long tail for sewing, and set aside.

Head

Rnd 1: Using G hook and black yarn, ch 2, 6 sc in second ch from hook.
Rnd 2: Sc 2 in each sc around. (12 sts)
Rnd 3: *Sc 1, 2 sc in next sc*, rep 6 times. (18 sts)
Rnd 4: *Sc 2, 2 sc in next sc*, rep 6 times. (24 sts)
Rnd 5: *Sc 3, 2 sc in next sc*, rep 6 times. (30 sts)
Rnd 6: *Sc 4, 2 sc in next sc*, rep 6 times. (36 sts)
Rnd 7: *Sc 5, 2 sc in next sc*, rep 6 times. (42 sts)
Rnds 8–19: Sc 42.
Rnd 20: *Sc 5, dec 1*, rep 6 times. (36 sts)
Rnd 21: *Sc 4, dec 1*, rep 6 times. (30 sts)
Insert eyes into roundies, attach eyes to head, and sew roundies to head. Stuff beak and sew to head.
Rnd 22: Sc 30.
Rnd 23: *Sc 3, dec 1*, rep 6 times. (24 sts)
Rnd 24: *Sc 2, dec 1*, rep 6 times. (18 sts)

Stuff head firmly.
Rnd 25: *Sc 1, dec 1*, rep 6 times. (12 sts)
Fasten off and weave in ends.

Belly Spot

Rnd 1: Using G hook and white yarn, ch 2, 6 sc in second ch from hook.
Rnd 2: Sc 2 in each sc around. (12 sts)
Rnd 3: *Sc 1, 2 sc in next sc*, rep 6 times. (18 sts)
Rnd 4: *Sc 4 in next sc, sc 8*, rep twice. (24 sts)
Rnd 5: *Dc 4, hdc 8*, rep twice. (24 sts)
Fasten off, leaving a long tail for sewing, and set aside.

Body

Rnd 1: Using G hook and black yarn, ch 2, 6 sc in second ch from hook.

Rnd 2: Sc 2 in each sc around. (12 sts)

Rnd 3: *Sc 1, 2 sc in next sc*, rep 6 times. (18 sts)

Rnd 4: *Sc 2, 2 sc in next sc*, rep 6 times. (24 sts)

Rnd 5: *Sc 3, 2 sc in next sc*, rep 6 times. (30 sts)

Rnd 6: *Sc 4, 2 sc in next sc*, rep 6 times. (36 sts)

Rnd 7: *Sc 5, 2 sc in next sc*, rep 6 times. (42 sts)

Rnd 8: *Sc 6, 2 sc in next sc*, rep 6 times. (48 sts)

Rnds 9–14: Sc 48.

Rnd 15: *Sc 6, dec 1*, rep 6 times. (42 sts)

Rnd 16: Sc 42.

Rnd 17: *Sc 5, dec 1*, rep 6 times. (36 sts)

Rnds 18–20: Sc 36.

Rnd 21: *Sc 4, dec 1*, rep 6 times. (30 sts)

Rnds 22–25: Sc 30.

Rnd 26: *Sc 3, dec 1*, rep 6 times. (24 sts)

Rnd 27: Sc 24.

Fasten off, leaving a long tail for sewing. Sew belly spot to body, stuff body firmly, and sew to head.

Feet

Make 2.

Rnd 1: Using G hook and yellow yarn, ch 2, 8 sc in second ch from hook.

Rnd 2: Sc 2 in each sc around. (16 sts)

Rnds 3–8: Sc 16.

Fasten off, leaving a long tail for sewing. Stuff, sew open end closed, and sew foot to body. Make sure to sew feet almost to edge of body so your penguin can stand by herself.

Wings

Make 2.

Rnd 1: Using G hook and black yarn, ch 2, 7 sc in second ch from hook.

Rnd 2: Sc 2 in each sc around. (14 sts)

Rnds 3–13: Sc 14.

Rnd 14: *Sk 1 sc, sc 1*, rep 7 times. (7 sts)

Fasten off, leaving a long tail for sewing. Sew open end closed and sew to body (no need to stuff wings).

Baby

Eye Roundies

Make 2.

Rnd 1: Using F hook and blue yarn, ch 2, 6 sc in second ch from hook.

Rnd 2: Sc 2 in each sc around. (12 sts)

Fasten off, leaving a long tail for sewing, and set aside.

Beak

Rnd 1: Using F hook and yellow yarn, ch 2, 4 sc in second ch from hook.

Rnd 2: Sc 2 in each sc around. (8 sts)

Rnd 3: Sc 8.

Rnd 4: *Sc 1, 2 sc in next sc*, rep 4 times. (12 sts)

Rnd 5: Sc 12.

Fasten off, leaving a long tail for sewing, and set aside.

Head

Rnd 1: Using G hook and black yarn, ch 2, 6 sc in second ch from hook.

Rnd 2: Sc 2 in each sc around. (12 sts)

Rnd 3: *Sc 1, 2 sc in next sc*, rep 6 times. (18 sts)

Rnd 4: *Sc 2, 2 sc in next sc*, rep 6 times. (24 sts)

Rnd 5: *Sc 3, 2 sc in next sc*, rep 6 times. (30 sts)

Rnds 6–14: Sc 30.

Rnd 15: *Sc 3, dec 1*, rep 6 times. (24 sts)

Insert eyes into roundies, attach eyes to head, and sew roundies to head. Stuff beak and sew to head.

Rnd 16: *Sc 2, dec 1*, rep 6 times. (18 sts)

Rnd 17: Sc 18.

Stuff head firmly.

Rnd 18: *Sc 1, dec 1*, rep 6 times. (12 sts)

Fasten off and weave in ends.

Belly Spot

Rnd 1: Using G hook and white yarn, ch 2, 6 sc in second ch from hook.

Rnd 2: Sc 2 in each sc around. (12 sts)

Rnd 3: *3 sc in next sc, sc 5*, rep twice. (16 sts)

Fasten off, leaving a long tail for sewing, and set aside.

Body

Rnd 1: Using G hook and black yarn, ch 2, 6 sc in second ch from hook.

Rnd 2: Sc 2 in each sc around. (12 sts)

Rnd 3: *Sc 1, 2 sc in next sc*, rep 6 times. (18 sts)

Rnd 4: *Sc 2, 2 sc in next sc*, rep 6 times. (24 sts)

Rnd 5: *Sc 3, 2 sc in next sc*, rep 6 times. (30 sts)

Rnd 6: *Sc 4, 2 sc in next sc*, rep 6 times. (36 sts)

Rnds 7–9: Sc 36.

Rnd 10: *Sc 4, dec 1*, rep 6 times. (30 sts)

Rnd 11: *Sc 3, dec 1*, rep 6 times. (24 sts)

Rnd 12: *Sc 2, dec 1*, rep 6 times. (18 sts)

Rnds 13–15: Sc 18.

Fasten off, leaving a long tail for sewing. Sew belly spot to body, stuff body firmly, and sew to head.

Feet

Make 2.

Rnd 1: Using G hook and yellow yarn, ch 2, 5 sc in second ch from hook.

Rnd 2: Sc 2 in each sc around. (10 sts)

Rnds 3–5: Sc 10.

Fasten off, leaving a long tail for sewing. Stuff, sew open end closed, and sew to body. Make sure you sew feet almost to the edge of body so your penguin can stand by herself.

Wings

Make 2.

Rnd 1: Using G hook and black yarn, ch 2, 4 sc in second ch from hook.

Rnd 2: Sc 2 in each sc around. (8 sts)

Rnds 3–9: Sc 8.

Fasten off, leaving a long tail for sewing. Sew open end closed and sew to body (no need to stuff wings).

Baby Owl and Her Mommy

A family of burrowing owls used to live in my backyard when I was growing up, and I always wanted to bring a couple of them inside to play with me. I told my daughter Oli the story and this little pair followed.

Finished Sizes

Mommy: Approx 4½" tall
Baby: Approx 3" tall

Materials

Worsted-weight yarn in brown, gold, tan, and orange
Size G-6 (4 mm) crochet hook
9 mm plastic eyes with safety backings
Tapestry needle
Fiberfill or stuffing of your choice

Mommy

Eye Roundies

Make 2.
Rnd 1: Using gold yarn, ch 3, 6 hdc in third ch from hook.
Rnd 2: Hdc 2 in each hdc around. (12 sts)
Rnd 3: *Sc 1, 2 sc in next hdc*, rep 6 times. (18 sts)
Fasten off, leaving a long tail for sewing. Set aside.

Body

Rnd 1: Using brown yarn, ch 2, 6 sc in second ch from hook.
Rnd 2: Sc 2 in each sc around. (12 sts)
Rnd 3: *Sc 1, 2 sc in next sc*, rep 6 times. (18 sts)
Rnd 4: *Sc 2, 2 sc in next sc*, rep 6 times. (24 sts)
Rnd 5: *Sc 3, 2 sc in next sc*, rep 6 times. (30 sts)
Rnd 6: *Sc 4, 2 sc in next sc*, rep 6 times. (36 sts)
Rnds 7–12: Sc 36.
Rnds 13–18: Change to tan yarn, sc 36.
Insert eyes into roundies, attach eyes to head, and sew roundies to head. Embroider beak using orange yarn.

Rnd 19: *Sc 5, 2 sc in next sc*, rep 6 times. (42 sts)

Rnds 20–28: Sc 42.

Rnd 29: *Sc 5, dec 1*, rep 6 times. (36 sts)

Rnd 30: *Sc 4, dec 1*, rep 6 times. (30 sts)

Rnd 31: *Sc 3, dec 1*, rep 6 times. (24 sts)

Rnd 32: *Sc 2, dec 1*, rep 6 times. (18 sts)

Rnd 33: *Sc 1, dec 1*, rep 6 times. (12 sts)

Stuff body.

Rnd 34: *Sk 1 sc, sc 1*, rep 6 times. (6 sts)

Fasten off and weave in ends.

Wings

Make 2.

Rnd 1: Using gold yarn, ch 2, 6 sc in second ch from hook.

Rnd 2: Sc 2 in each sc around. (12 sts)

Rnds 3–10: Sc 12.

Fasten off, leaving a long tail for sewing. Sew open end closed and sew to body (no need to stuff wings).

Baby

Eye Roundies

Make 2.

Rnd 1: Using gold yarn, ch 3, 6 hdc in third ch from hook.

Rnd 2: Sc 2 in each hdc around. (12 sts)

Fasten off, leaving a long tail for sewing. Set aside.

Body

Rnd 1: Using brown yarn, ch 2, 6 sc in second ch from hook.

Rnd 2: Sc 2 in each sc around. (12 sts)

Rnd 3: *Sc 1, 2 sc in next sc*, rep 6 times. (18 sts)

Rnd 4: *Sc 2, 2 sc in next sc*, rep 6 times. (24 sts)

Rnds 5–8: Sc 24.

Rnds 9–14: Change to tan yarn, sc 24.

Insert eyes into roundies, attach eyes to head, and sew roundies to head. Embroider beak with orange yarn.

Rnd 15: *Sc 3, 2 sc in next sc*, rep 6 times. (30 sts)

Rnds 16–18: Sc 30.

Rnd 19: *Sc 3, dec 1*, rep 6 times. (24 sts)

Rnd 20: *Sc 2, dec 1*, rep 6 times. (18 sts)

Rnd 21: *Sc 1, dec 1*, rep 6 times. (12 sts)

Stuff body.

Rnd 22: *Sk 1 sc, sc 1*, rep 6 times. (6 sts)

Fasten off and weave in ends.

Wings

Make 2.

Rnd 1: Using brown yarn, ch 2, 5 sc in second ch from hook.

Rnd 2: Sc 2 in each sc around. (10 sts)

Rnds 3–7: Sc 10.

Fasten off, leaving a long tail for sewing. Sew open end closed and sew to body (no need to stuff wings).

Baby Hedgehog and Her Mommy

Hedgehogs remind me of little babies, all cute and cuddly and shy. Mine, however, turned out like little disco kids. Don't they remind you of the '70s, with their hair and carefree look?

Finished Sizes

Mommy: Approx 4½" tall
Baby: Approx 3" tall

Materials

Worsted-weight yarn in tan and brown
Size G-6 (4 mm) crochet hook
6 mm and 9 mm plastic eyes with safety backings
Black and red embroidery floss and sharp needle
Fiberfill or stuffing of your choice
2 small decorative buttons or beads

Mommy

Muzzle

Rnd 1: Using tan yarn, ch 2, 5 sc in second ch from hook.
Rnd 2: Sc 2 in each sc around. (10 sts)
Rnd 3: *Sc 1, 2 sc in next sc*, rep 5 times. (15 sts)
Rnd 4: Sc 15.
Fasten off, leaving a long tail for sewing.
Embroider nose and mouth and set aside.

Head and Body

Rnd 1: Using tan yarn, ch 2, 8 sc in second ch from hook.
Rnd 2: Sc 2 in each sc around. (16 sts)
Rnd 3: *Sc 1, 2 sc in next sc*, rep 8 times. (24 sts)
Rnd 4: *Sc 2, 2 sc in next sc*, rep 8 times. (32 sts)
Rnd 5: *Sc 3, 2 sc in next sc*, rep 8 times. (40 sts)
Rnds 6–17: Sc 40.
Rnd 18: *Sc 6, dec 1*, rep 5 times. (35 sts)
Rnd 19: *Sc 5, dec 1*, rep 5 times. (30 sts)
Rnds 20–22: Sc 30.
Rnd 23: *Sc 4, dec 1*, rep 5 times. (25 sts)
Rnd 24: Sc 25.
Rnd 25: *Sc 3, dec 1*, rep 5 times. (20 sts)
Sew muzzle in place and attach 9 mm eyes.
Rnd 26: *Sc 2, dec 1*, rep 5 times. (15 sts)
Stuff body.
Rnd 27: *Sc 1, dec 1*, rep 5 times. (10 sts)
Rnd 28: *Sk 1 sc, sc 1*, rep 5 times. (5 sts)
Fasten off and weave in ends.

Ears

Make 2.
Using tan yarn, ch 3, 6 dc in third ch from hook.
Fasten off, leaving long tail for sewing.
Fold in half, sew bottom part tog (so ears look like little mouse ears), and sew to head.

Prickly Coat

Using brown yarn, join yarn at a sc on bottom of back of body. Get ready; this takes forever! Work in rows all over the back and on top of the head as follows: *Ch 3, sk 2 sc, sc 1, rep from *.
Fasten off and weave in ends.

Arms

Make 2.
Rnd 1: Using tan yarn, ch 2, 5 sc in second ch from hook.
Rnd 2: 2 sc in each sc around. (10 sts)
Rnds 3–8: Sc 10.
Fasten off, leaving long tail for sewing. Stuff lightly and sew to body.

Finishing

If adding a decorative button or bead, use 2 strands of embroidery floss to stitch it to Mommy Hedgehog's head, referring to the photo on page 33 for placement.

Baby

Muzzle

Rnd 1: Using tan yarn, ch 2, 5 sc in second ch from hook.
Rnd 2: Sc 2 in each sc around. (10 sts)
Rnd 3: Sc 10.
Fasten off, leaving a long tail for sewing. Embroider nose and mouth and set aside.

Head and Body

Rnd 1: Using tan yarn, ch 2, 8 sc in second ch from hook.
Rnd 2: Sc 2 in each sc around. (16 sts)
Rnd 3: *Sc 1, 2 sc in next sc*, rep 8 times. (24 sts)
Rnds 4–10: Sc 24.
Rnd 11: *Sc 4, dec 1*, rep 4 times. (20 sts)
Rnds 12 and 13: Sc 20.
Rnd 14: *Sc 3, dec 1*, rep 4 times. (16 sts)
Sew muzzle in place and attach 6 mm eyes.
Rnd 15: *Sc 2, dec 1*, rep 4 times. (12 sts)
Stuff body.
Rnd 16: *Sc 1, dec 1*, rep 4 times. (8 sts)
Rnd 17: *Sk 1 sc, sc 1*, rep 4 times. (4 sts)
Fasten off and weave in ends.

Ears

Make 2.
Using tan yarn, ch 2, 7 sc in third ch from hook.
Fasten off, leaving long tail for sewing.
Fold ears in half, sew bottom part tog (so ears look like little mouse ears), and sew to head.

Prickly Coat

Work as for Mommy (page 34).

Arms

Make 2.
Rnd 1: Using tan yarn, ch 2, 3 sc in second ch from hook.
Rnd 2: Sc 2 in each sc around. (6 sts)
Rnds 3–6: Sc 6.
Fasten off, leaving long tail for sewing. Stuff lightly and sew to body.

Finishing

If adding a decorative button or bead, use 2 strands of embroidery floss to stitch it to Baby Hedgehog's palm (inside of arm), referring to the photo below for placement.

Boy and Girl Elephants

Villa Dolores is Montevideo's zoo, and for the longest time, Leo the baby elephant was its most visited and popular resident. Children all drew pictures of him and visited and brought him peanuts. My drawings always involved a long scarf and a friend with a tutu, so here's Leo and friend in their softie versions.

Finished Size

Approx 7" tall

Materials

Worsted-weight yarn in gray, pink, white, and green
Size G-6 (4 mm) crochet hook
9 mm plastic eyes with safety backings
Small pieces of white craft felt
Sewing thread and sharp needle
Black embroidery floss and tapestry needle
Fiberfill or stuffing of your choice

Boy or Girl Elephant

Use gray yarn if making boy and pink yarn if making girl.

Trunk

Rnd 1: Ch 2, 6 sc in second ch from hook.
Rnd 2: Sc 2 in each sc around. (12 sts)
Rnds 3–7: Sc 12.
Rnd 8: Hdc 6 through back loops only, sc 6.
Rnds 9–12: Sc 12.
Rnd 13: *Sc 1, 2 sc in next sc*, rep 6 times. (18 sts)
Rnd 14: Sc 18.
Fasten off, leaving a long tail for sewing. Stuff and set aside.

Head

Rnd 1: Ch 2, 6 sc in second ch from hook.
Rnd 2: Sc 2 in each sc around. (12 sts)
Rnd 3: *Sc 1, 2 sc in next sc*, rep 6 times. (18 sts)
Rnd 4: *Sc 2, 2 sc in next sc*, rep 6 times. (24 sts)
Rnd 5: *Sc 3, 2 sc in next sc*, rep 6 times. (30 sts)
Rnd 6: *Sc 4, 2 sc in next sc*, rep 6 times. (36 sts)
Rnd 7: *Sc 5, 2 sc in next sc*, rep 6 times. (42 sts)
Rnds 8–18: Sc 42.
Sew trunk to head. Cut 2 elephant eyes from white felt using the pattern on page 39. Cut a small slit in middle of each circle, insert eyes, and secure to head. Sew circles to head.
Rnd 19: *Sc 5, dec 1*, rep 6 times. (36 sts)
Rnd 20: *Sc 4, dec 1*, rep 6 times. (30 sts)
Rnd 21: Sc 30.
Rnd 22: *Sc 3, dec 1*, rep 6 times. (24 sts)
Rnd 23: *Sc 2, dec 1*, rep 6 times. (18 sts)
Stuff head firmly.
Rnd 24: *Sc 1, dec 1*, rep 6 times. (12 sts)
Rnd 25: *Sk 1 sc, sc 1*, rep 6 times. (6 sts)
Fasten off and weave in ends.

Ears

Make 2.

Rnd 1: Ch 2, 6 sc in second ch from hook.

Rnd 2: 2 sc in each sc around. (12 sts)

Rnd 3: *Sc 1, 2 sc in next sc*, rep 6 times. (18 sts)

Rnd 4: *Sc 2, 2 sc in next sc*, rep 6 times. (24 sts)

Rnds 5–10: Sc 24.

Rnd 11: *Sc 2, dec 1*, rep 6 times. (18 sts)

Rnd 12: Sc 18.

Rnd 13: *Sc 1, dec 1*, rep 6 times. (12 sts)

Rnds 14–15: Sc 12.

Fasten off, leaving a long tail for sewing. Sew open end closed and sew to head.

Body

Rnd 1: Ch 2, 6 sc in second ch from hook.

Rnd 2: Sc 2 in each sc around. (12 sts)

Rnd 3: *Sc 1, 2 sc in next sc*, rep 6 times. (18 sts)

Rnd 4: *Sc 2, 2 sc in next sc*, rep 6 times. (24 sts)

Rnd 5: *Sc 3, 2 sc in next sc*, rep 6 times. (30 sts)

Rnds 6–8: Sc 30.

For Girl only:

Rnd 9: Sc 30 through back loops only. (You'll use the front loops later when crocheting the skirt.)

For Boy only:

Rnd 9: Sc 30.

For both:

Rnd 10: *Sc 3, dec 1*, rep 6 times. (24 sts)

Rnds 11–15: Sc 24.

Fasten off, leaving a long tail for sewing. Stuff and sew to body.

Skirt for Girl

Holding doll upside down (legs up in the air), join white yarn at back to one of the front loops you left in rnd 9 when making body.

Rnd 1: Sc 30 through the front loops all around body.

Rnd 2: Sc 2 in each sc around. (60 sts)

Rnd 3: Sc 60.

Rep rnd 3 until you're happy with the skirt length.

Fasten off and weave in ends.

Legs and Arms

Make 2 of each.

Rnd 1: Ch 2, 6 sc in second ch from hook.

Rnd 2: Sc 2 in each sc around. (12 sts)

Rnd 3: *Sc 1, 2 sc in next sc*, rep 6 times. (18 sts)

Rnd 4: *Sc 2, 2 sc in next sc*, rep 6 times. (24 sts)

Rnd 5: Through back loops only, *sc 2, dec 1*, rep 6 times. (18 sts)

Rnd 6: *Sc 1, dec 1*, rep 6 times. (12 sts)

Rnd 7: Sc 12.

Using pattern on this page, cut 2 toenail pieces from felt and sew to top of foot referring to photo on page 36 for placement.

Rnds 8–11: Sc 12.

Fasten off, leaving a long tail for sewing. Stuff arms, sew open end closed, and sew to body. Stuff legs and sew to body.

Tail

Ch 5. Starting in second ch from hook, sl 1 st, sc 1, hdc 1, dc 1.

Fasten off, leaving long tail for sewing, and sew to body.

Scarf for Boy

Using green yarn, loosely ch 80, turn.

Row 1: Ch 2, hdc in third ch from hook and in each ch across, turn.

Row 2: Hdc 80.

Fasten off and weave in loose ends.

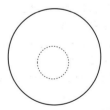

Elephant eye

Elephant toenails

Baby Octopus and Her Mommy

The octopi were the first in a moms and babies series I started right after my daughter Martina was born. I figured that with a newborn and a three-year-old I would actually need eight arms to be able to hug them both as many times as I wanted to—and to keep up with the housework.

Finished Sizes

Mommy: Approx 3" when sitting
Baby: Approx 2¼" when sitting

Materials

Worsted-weight yarn in purple and blue, or in desired colors
Size F-5 (4 mm) crochet hook
9 mm plastic eyes with safety backings
Small pieces of red and pink craft felt
Sewing thread and sharp needle
Black embroidery floss and tapestry needle
Fiberfill or stuffing of your choice

Mommy

Head and Body

Rnd 1: Using purple yarn, ch 2, 6 sc in second chain from hook.
Rnd 2: Sc 2 in each sc around. (12 sts)
Rnd 3: *Sc 1, 2 sc in next sc*, rep 6 times. (18 sts)
Rnd 4: *Sc 2, 2 sc in next sc*, rep 6 times. (24 sts)
Rnd 5: *Sc 3, 2 sc in next sc*, rep 6 times. (30 sts)
Rnd 6: *Sc 4, 2 sc in next sc*, rep 6 times. (36 sts)
Rnd 7: *Sc 5, 2 sc in next sc*, rep 6 times. (42 sts)
Rnds 8–18: Sc 42.
Rnd 19: *Sc 5, dec 1*, rep 6 times. (36 sts)
Rnd 20: *Sc 4, dec 1*, rep 6 times. (30 sts)
Rnds 21–22: Sc 30.
Attach eyes and embroider mouth. For cheeks, cut 2 circles from red felt using pattern on page 42 and sew to head.

Rnd 23: *Sc 3, dec 1*, rep 6 times. (24 sts)
Rnd 24: *Sc 2, dec 1*, rep 6 times. (18 sts)
Stuff body almost to top.
Rnd 25: *Sc 1, dec 1*, rep 6 times. (12 sts)
Finish stuffing.
Rnd 26: *Sk 1 sc, sc 1*, rep 6 times. (6 sts)
Fasten off and weave in ends.

Arms

Make 8.
Rnd 1: Ch 2, 4 sc in second chain from hook.

Rnd 2: Sc 2 in each sc around. (8 sts)

Rnds 3–11: Sc 8, stuffing as you go.

Fasten off, leaving a long tail for sewing. After all eight arms are finished, sew them evenly around the body.

Baby

Head and Body

Rnd 1: Ch 2, 6 sc in second chain from hook.

Rnd 2: Sc 2 in each sc around. (12 sts)

Rnd 3: *Sc 1, 2 sc in next sc*, rep 6 times. (18 sts)

Rnd 4: *Sc 2, 2 sc in next sc*, rep 6 times. (24 sts)

Rnd 5: *Sc 3, 2 sc in next sc*, rep 6 times. (30 sts)

Rnds 6–11: Sc 30.

Rnd 12: *Sc 3, dec 1*, rep 6 times. (24 sts)

Rnds 13–15: Sc 24.

Attach eyes and embroider mouth. For cheeks, cut 2 circles from pink felt using pattern below right and sew to head.

Rnd 16: *Sc 2, dec 1*, rep 6 times. (18 sts)

Stuff body almost to top.

Rnd 17: *Sc 1, dec 1*, rep 6 times. (12 sts)

Finish stuffing.

Rnd 18: *Sk 1 sc, sc 1*, rep 6 times. (6 sts)

Fasten off and weave in ends.

Arms

Make 8.

Rnd 1: Ch 2, 3 sc in second chain from hook.

Rnd 2: Sc 2 in each sc around. (6 sts)

Rnds 3–6: Sc 6, stuffing as you go.

Fasten off, leaving a long tail for sewing. After all eight arms are finished, sew them evenly around the body.

Octopus cheek

These eggs are a definite favorite among kids and grown-ups! My daughter Oli and her friends love to see what's inside the eggs and they spend a lot of time taking them out of the egg carton and reorganizing them.

Finished Sizes

Whole egg: Approx 2½" tall
Eggshell bottom: Approx 1½" tall
Eggshell top: Approx 1¼" tall
Chick: Approx 1¾" tall

Materials

Worsted-weight yarn in white, gold, and orange
Size F-5 (3.75 mm) and E-4 (3.5 mm) crochet hooks
6 mm plastic eyes with safety backings
Small pieces of tan craft felt
Sewing thread and sharp needle
Black embroidery floss and tapestry needle
Fiberfill or stuffing of your choice

Whole Egg

Rnd 1: Using F hook and white yarn, ch 2, 5 sc in second ch from hook.
Rnd 2: Sc 2 in each sc around. (10 sts)
Rnd 3: *Sc 1, 2 sc in next sc*, rep 5 times. (15 sts)
Rnd 4: Sc 15.
Rnd 5: *Sc 2, 2 sc in next sc*, rep 5 times. (20 sts)

Rnd 6: *Sc 3, 2 sc in next sc*, rep 5 times. (25 sts)
Rnds 7–13: Sc 25.
Rnd 14: *Sc 3, dec 1*, rep 5 times. (20 sts)
Attach eyes and embroider mouth. For cheeks, cut 2 circles from felt using pattern on page 45 and sew in place.
Rnd 15: *Sc 2, dec 1*, rep 5 times. (15 sts)
Rnd 16: Sc 15.
Stuff.
Rnd 17: *Sc 1, dec 1*, rep 5 times. (10 sts)
Rnd 18: *Sk 1 sc, sc 1*, rep 5 times. (5 sts)
Fasten off and weave in ends.

Eggshell Bottom

Rnd 1: Using F hook and white yarn, ch 2, 5 sc in second ch from hook.
Rnd 2: Sc 2 in each sc around. (10 sts)
Rnd 3: *Sc 1, 2 sc in next sc*, rep 5 times. (15 sts)
Rnd 4: Sc 15.
Rnd 5: *Sc 2, 2 sc in next sc*, rep 5 times. (20 sts)
Rnd 6: *Sc 3, 2 sc in next sc*, rep 5 times. (25 sts)

Rnds 7–9: Sc 25.
Rnd 10: BPsc 25.
Rnd 11: *Sc 3, dec 1*, rep 5 times. (20 sts)
Rnd 12: Sc 20, sl st in next sc.
Fasten off and weave in ends.

Eggshell Top

Rnd 1: Using F hook and white yarn, ch 2, 5 sc in second ch from hook.
Rnd 2: Sc 2 in each sc around. (10 sts)
Rnd 3: *Sc 1, 2 sc in next sc*, rep 5 times. (15 sts)
Rnd 4: Sc 15.
Rnd 5: *Sc 2, 2 sc in next sc*, rep 5 times. (20 sts)
Rnd 6: *Sc 3, 2 sc in next sc*, rep 5 times. (25 sts)
Rnds 7–10: Sc 25.
Fasten off and weave in ends.

Chick

Rnd 1: Using E hook and gold or orange yarn, ch 2, 5 sc in second ch from hook.
Rnd 2: Sc 2 in each sc around. (10 sts)
Rnd 3: *Sc 1, 2 sc in next sc*, rep 5 times. (15 sts)

Rnd 4: *Sc 2, 2 sc in next sc*, rep 5 times. (20 sts)

Rnds 5–10: Sc 20.

Attach eyes. Using pattern right, cut beak from felt and sew in place.

Rnd 11: *Sc 2, dec 1*, rep 5 times. (15 sts)

Rnd 12: Sc 15.

Stuff almost to top.

Rnd 13: *Sc 1, dec 1*, rep 5 times. (10 sts)

Finish stuffing.

Rnd 14: *Sk 1 sc, sc 1*, rep 5 times. (5 sts)

Fasten off and weave in ends.

Stitching line ⟶

Chick beak　　**Egg cheek**

Smiling Desserts

What could be better than a smiling dessert? I bet you they're smiling because you can make as many cupcakes and ice-cream cones and *café con leche* cups as you want and never, ever grow tired of looking at them . . . and they know it. (They make great pincushions, too!)

Finished Sizes

***Café con leche* cup:** Approx 1¾" tall
Cupcake: Approx 2" tall
Ice-cream cone: Approx 3¼" tall

Materials

Worsted-weight yarn in blue, tan, bright pink, light pink, and brown
Size F-5 (4 mm) crochet hook
6 mm plastic eyes with safety backings
Small piece of pink craft felt
Sewing thread and sharp needle
Black embroidery floss and tapestry needle
Small seed beads in assorted colors for cupcake
Fiberfill or stuffing of your choice

Café con Leche Cup

Rnd 1: Using blue yarn, ch 2, 7 sc in second ch from hook.
Rnd 2: Sc 2 in each sc around. (14 sts)
Rnd 3: *Sc 1, 2 sc in next sc*, rep 7 times. (21 sts)
Rnd 4: *Sc 2, 2 sc in next sc*, rep 7 times. (28 sts)

Rnd 5: *Sc 3, 2 sc in next sc*, rep 7 times. (35 sts)
Rnd 6: Through back loops only, *sc 3, dec 1*, rep 7 times. (28 sts)
Rnds 7–15: Sc 28.
Fasten off and weave in ends.
Attach eyes and embroider mouth. For cheeks, cut 2 circles of pink felt using pattern on page 49 and sew in place.

Handle

Using blue yarn, ch 14, hdc 12 starting in third ch from hook.
Fasten off, leaving long tail for sewing. Weave in ends and sew to mug.

Café con Leche

Rnd 1: Using tan yarn, ch 2, 5 sc in second ch from hook.
Rnd 2: Sc 2 in each sc around. (10 sts)

Rnd 3: *Sc 1, 2 sc in next sc*, rep 5 times. (15 sts)

Rnd 4: *Sc 2, 2 sc in next sc*, rep 5 times. (20 sts)

Rnd 5: *Sc 3, 2 sc in next sc*, rep 5 times. (25 sts)

Stuff mug and sew café con leche to inside of mug, about ½" below rim.

Cupcake

Bottom

Rnd 1: Using tan yarn, ch 2, 6 sc in second ch from hook.

Rnd 2: Sc 2 in each sc around. (12 sts)

Rnd 3: *Sc 1, 2 sc in next sc*, rep 6 times. (18 sts)

Rnd 4: *Sc 2, 2 sc in next sc*, rep 6 times. (24 sts)

Rnd 5: *Sc 3, 2 sc in next sc*, rep 6 times. (30 sts)

Rnd 6: Through back loops only, *sc 3, dec 1*, rep 6 times. (24 sts)

Rnd 7: *Sc 3, 2 sc in next sc*, rep 6 times. (30 sts)

Rnds 8–11: Sc 30.

Fasten off, leaving a long tail for sewing, and set aside.

Attach eyes and embroider mouth.

Icing

Rnd 1: Using light-pink yarn, ch 2, 6 sc in second ch from hook.

Rnd 2: Sc 2 in each sc around. (12 sts)

Rnd 3: *Sc 1, 2 sc in next sc*, rep 6 times. (18 sts)

Rnd 4: *Sc 2, 2 sc in next sc*, rep 6 times. (24 sts)

Rnd 5: *Sc 3, 2 sc in next sc*, rep 6 times. (30 sts)

Rnds 6–9: Sc 30.

Rnd 10: *Sc 4 in next sc, sk 1 sc, sl st 1*, rep 10 times.

Fasten off and weave in ends. Using a sharp needle and sewing thread, sew seed bead "sprinkles" to icing.

Finishing

Place the icing on top of the cupcake, lining up the stitches of the cupcake bottom with the stitches inside the wavy edge of the icing. Sew three-quarters of the way around (don't sew into the wavy part), and then stuff the bottom with fiberfill so the cupcake sits nice and flat. Stuff both the cupcake and icing with fiberfill. Finish sewing all the way around.

Ice-Cream Cone

Cone

Rnd 1: Using tan yarn, ch 2, sc 4 in second ch from hook.

Rnd 2: Sc 4.

Rnd 3: *Sc 1, 2 sc in next sc*, rep twice. (6 sts)

Rnd 4: Sc 6.

Rnd 5: *Sc 1, 2 sc in next sc*, rep 3 times. (9 sts)

Rnd 6: Sc 9.

Rnd 7: *Sc 2, 2 sc in next sc*, rep 3 times. (12 sts)

Rnd 8: *Sc 1, 2 sc in next sc*, rep 6 times. (18 sts)

Rnds 9–11: Sc 18, sl st to first st of rnd.

Fasten off, leaving a long tail for sewing, and set aside.

Ice Cream

Rnd 1: Using bright pink yarn, ch 2, 6 sc in second ch from hook.

Rnd 2: Sc 2 in each sc around. (12 sts)

Rnd 3: *Sc 1, 2 sc in next sc*, rep 6 times. (18 sts)

Rnd 4: *Sc 2, 2 sc in next sc*, rep 6 times. (24 sts)

Rnd 5: *Sc 3, 2 sc in next sc*, rep 6 times. (30 sts)

Rnds 6–12: Sc 30.

Rnd 13: *Sc 3, dec 1*, rep 6 times. (24 sts)

Attach eyes and embroider mouth.

Rnd 14: *Sc 2, dec 1*, rep 6 times. (18 sts)

Stuff almost full.

Rnd 15: *Sc 1, dec 1*, rep 6 times. (12 sts)

Finish stuffing, fasten off, and weave in ends. Stuff cone and sew to ice cream.

Chocolate Topping

Rnd 1: Using brown yarn, ch 2, 6 sc in second ch from hook.

Rnd 2: Sc 2 in each sc around. (12 sts)

Rnd 3: *Sc 1, 2 sc in next sc*, rep 6 times. (18 sts)

Rnd 4: *Sc 2, 2 sc in next sc*, rep 6 times. (24 sts)

Rnd 5: Sc 24.

Rnd 6: *Hdc 3 in next sc, sk 1 sc, sl st in next sc*, rep 8 times.

Fasten off, leaving a long tail for sewing, and sew to top of ice cream.

Cup cheek

Fruity Friends

How many times can a kid hear "eat your fruit"? Maybe we should start saying "hug your fruit." Who knows, befriending a pear or apple might be the beginning of a wonderful, fruity friendship.

Finished Size

Pear: Approx 3" tall
Apple: Approx 3" wide x 2" tall

Materials

Worsted-weight yarn in green, red, and brown
Size F-5 (4 mm) crochet hook
9 mm (2 sets) and 6 mm (1 set) plastic eyes with safety backings
Small pieces of pink craft felt
Sewing thread and sharp needle
Black embroidery floss and tapestry needle
Fiberfill or stuffing of your choice

Pear

Pear is worked from the bottom up. (Keep that in mind when working on the face.)

Rnd 1: With green yarn, ch 2, 6 sc in second ch from hook.
Rnd 2: Sc 2 in each sc around. (12 sts)
Rnd 3: *Sc 1, 2 sc in next sc*, rep 6 times. (18 sts)
Rnd 4: *Sc 2, 2 sc in next sc*, rep 6 times. (24 sts)
Rnd 5: *Sc 3, 2 sc in next sc*, rep 6 times. (30 sts)
Rnd 6: *Sc 4, 2 sc in next sc*, rep 6 times. (36 sts)
Rnd 7: *Sc 5, 2 sc in next sc*, rep 6 times. (42 sts)
Rnds 8–16: Sc 42.
Rnd 17: *Sc 5, dec 1*, rep 6 times. (36 sts)
Rnd 18: *Sc 4, dec 1*, rep 6 times. (30 sts)
Rnds 19 and 20: Sc 30.
Attach eyes and embroider mouth. For cheeks, cut 2 circles from pink felt using pattern on page 52 and sew in place.
Rnd 21: *Sc 3, dec 1*, rep 6 times. (24 sts)
Rnds 22–24: Sc 24.
Rnd 25: *Sc 2, dec 1*, rep 6 times. (18 sts)
Stuff almost to top.
Rnd 26: *Sc 1, dec 1*, rep 6 times. (12 sts)
Finish stuffing.
Rnd 27: *Sk 1 sc, sc 1*, rep 6 times. (6 sts)
Fasten off and weave in ends.

Stem

Using brown yarn, ch 5, sc 4 starting at second ch from hook.
Fasten off, leaving a long tail for sewing, and sew to pear.

Leaf

Using brown yarn, ch 8, and starting at second bump (the bumps are on opposite side, or behind the braidlike ch where you usually crochet) from hook: *Sl st 1, sc 1, dc 1, tr 1, dc 1, sc 1, sl st 1*, rep once on opposite side (which now looks like regular sc because you crocheted in the bumps).

Fasten off, leaving a long tail for sewing, and sew to pear.

Pear cheek

Little Apple and Worm

Stem

Using brown yarn, ch 5, sc 4 starting at second ch from hook.
Fasten off, leaving a long tail for sewing, and set aside.

Leaf

Using green yarn, ch 8, and starting at second bump (the "bumps" are on the opposite side of, or behind, the braidlike ch where you usually crochet) from hook: *Sl st 1, sc 1, dc 1, tr 1, dc 1, sc 1, sl st 1*, rep on the opposite side (which now looks like regular sc because you crocheted in the bumps).
Fasten off, leaving a long tail for sewing, and set aside.

Apple

Rnd 1: Using red yarn, ch 2, 6 sc in second ch from hook.
Rnd 2: Sc 2 in each sc around. (12 sts)
Rnd 3: *Sc 1, 2 sc in next sc*, rep 6 times. (18 sts)
Rnd 4: *Sc 2, 2 sc in next sc*, rep 6 times. (24 sts)

Rnd 5: *Sc 3, 2 sc in next sc*, rep 6 times. (30 sts)
Rnd 6: *Sc 4, 2 sc in next sc*, rep 6 times. (36 sts)
Rnd 7: *Sc 5, 2 sc in next sc*, rep 6 times. (42 sts)
Rnds 8–17: Sc 42.
Rnd 18: *Sc 5, dec 1*, rep 6 times. (36 sts)
Rnd 19: *Sc 4, dec 1*, rep 6 times. (30 sts)
Rnd 20: *Sc 3, dec 1*, rep 6 times. (24 sts)
Attach 9 mm eyes and embroider mouth.
Sew stem and leaf to top of apple. (It's easier to attach them now when you can work from the inside.)
Rnd 21: *Sc 2, dec 1*, rep 6 times. (18 sts)
Rnd 22: Sc 18.
Stuff almost to top.

Rnd 23: *Sc 1, dec 1*, rep 6 times. (12 sts)
Finish stuffing.
Rnd 24: *Sk 1 sc, sc 1*, rep 6 times. (6 sts)
Fasten off, and weave in ends.

Worm

Rnd 1: Using green yarn, ch 2, 8 sc in second ch from hook.
Rnds 2–4: Sc 8.
Attach 6 mm eyes and embroider mouth.
Rnds 5 and 6: Sc 8, stuffing as you go.
Rnd 7: Sc 4 through back loops only, sc 4.
Rnd 8: Hdc 4, sc 4.
Rnd 9: Sc 4.
Fasten off, leaving a long tail for sewing, and sew to apple.

Happy Little Airplane

I love this smiley, softie toy plane. How cute would it look to hang a bunch of them from a child's bedroom ceiling? You could even make different sizes by making the body a little bit longer or shorter!

Finished Size

Approx 8" long

Materials

Worsted-weight yarn in red, black, and gray
Size G-6 (4 mm) crochet hook
15 mm plastic eyes with safety backings
Small pieces of white craft felt
Sewing thread and sharp needle
Black embroidery floss and tapestry needle
Fiberfill or stuffing of your choice

Propeller

Nose

Rnd 1: Using black yarn, ch 2, 5 sc in second ch from hook.
Rnd 2: Sc 2 in each sc around. (10 sts)
Rnds 3 and 4: Sc 10.
Fasten off and set aside.

Blades

Make 2.
Rnd 1: Using gray yarn, ch 2, 5 sc in second ch from hook.
Rnd 2: Sc 2 in each sc around. (10 sts)
Rnds 3–9: Sc 10.

Rnd 10: Dec 5 times, sl st 1. (5 sts)
Fasten off, leaving long tail for sewing. Sew open end closed and sew blades to opposite sides of nose. Stuff nose a little and set aside.

Plane

Rnd 1: Using red yarn, ch 2, 5 sc in second ch from hook.
Rnd 2: Sc 2 in each sc around. (10 sts)
Rnd 3: *Sc 1, 2 sc in next sc*, rep 5 times. (15 sts)
Rnd 4: *Sc 2, 2 sc in next sc*, rep 5 times. (20 sts)
Rnd 5: *Sc 3, 2 sc in next sc*, rep 5 times. (25 sts)
Rnd 6: *Sc 4, 2 sc in next sc*, rep 5 times. (30 sts)
Rnds 7 and 8: Sc 30.
Rnd 9: *Sc 5, 2 sc in next sc*, rep 5 times. (35 sts)
Rnds 10 and 11: Sc 35.
Rnd 12: *Sc 6, 2 sc in next sc*, rep 5 times. (40 sts)
Rnds 13–18: Sc 40.
Sew propeller to end of plane, position and attach eyes, embroider mouth.
Rnds 19–33: Sc 40.

Rnd 34: *Sc 6, dec 1*, rep 5 times. (35 sts)

Rnd 35: *Sc 5, dec 1*, rep 5 times. (30 sts)

Rnds 36 and 37: Sc 30.

Rnd 38: *Sc 4, dec 1*, rep 5 times. (25 sts)

Rnds 39 and 40: Sc 25.

Rnd 41: *Sc 3, dec 1*, rep 5 times. (20 sts)

Stuff almost to top.

Rnd 42: *Sc 2, dec 1*, rep 5 times. (15 sts)

Rnd 43: *Sc 1, dec 1*, rep 5 times. (10 sts)

Finish stuffing.

Rnd 44: *Sk 1 sc, sc 1*, rep 5 times. (5 sts)

Fasten off, leaving long tail. Thread tail onto tapestry needle and weave through rem 5 sts and pull tight to close hole. Weave in end.

Side Wings

Make 2.

Rnd 1: Using red yarn, ch 2, 8 sc in second ch from hook.

Rnd 2: Sc 2 in each sc around. (16 sts)

Rnds 3–15: Sc 16.

Fasten off, leaving long tail for sewing. Stuff lightly and sew to each side of plane.

Tail

Rnd 1: Using red yarn, ch 2, 7 sc in second ch from hook.

Rnd 2: Sc 2 in each sc around. (14 sts)

Rnds 3–8: Sc 14.

Fasten off, leaving long tail for sewing. Stuff lightly and sew to back of plane.

Back Wings

Make 2.

Rnd 1: Using red yarn, ch 2, 6 sc in second ch from hook.

Rnd 2: Sc 2 in each sc around. (12 sts)

Rnds 3–8: Sc 12.

Fasten off, leaving long tail for sewing. Stuff lightly and sew to each side at back of plane, below tail.

Finishing

Cut out 6 white felt windows using pattern below and sew or glue to airplane's body.

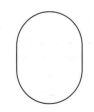

Airplane window

Branch Mobile

This mobile would look pretty in front of a window, with the light shining through it. You could even turn the birds into little hanging toys for a baby's car seat or a little kid's backpack. Just thread a piece of yarn through one of the stitches at the top of the head and knot the ends to form a loop.

Finished Size

Approx 36" from hanging ring

Materials

Worsted-weight yarn in brown, green, blue, and tiny amounts of white and yellow

Size F-5 (3.75 mm) and G-6 (4 mm) crochet hooks; use F hook unless stated otherwise

6 mm plastic eyes with safety backings

Small piece of tan craft felt for birds' beaks

Black embroidery floss and tapestry needle

Sewing thread and sharp needle

1 ring for hanging (mine is bamboo, approx 2½" in diameter)

Fiberfill or stuffing of your choice

Branch Mobile

Using G hook and brown yarn, loosely ch 101 and join first and last sts to form a ring, being careful not to twist sts.

Rnds 1–16: Sc 100.

Fasten off, leaving long tail for sewing. Fold edges together horizontally and sew to form a donut shape, stuffing as you go.

Little Leaves

Make as many as you want.

Using G hook and green yarn, loosely ch 7, and starting at second ch from hook, sc 1, dc 1, tr 2, dc 1, sc 1; fasten off and weave in ends.

Vine around Branch

Using G hook and green yarn, loosely ch 200; fasten off. Wrap around branch and sew in place with little leaves.

Vines for Birds

Make 4.

Using G hook and green yarn, loosely ch 7, and *starting at second ch from hook, sc 1, dc 1, tr 2, dc 1, sc 1, loosely ch 17*, rep from * to * 5 times, and starting at second ch from hook, sc 1, dc 1, tr 2, dc 1, sc 1. There will be 7 leaves on each vine. Fasten off and sew one end of leaf to branch.

Vines for Flowers

Make 4.

Using G hook and green yarn, (*loosely ch 7, and starting at second ch from hook, sc 1, dc 1, tr 2, dc 1, sc 1*, rep from * to * 1 more time, **loosely ch 17, and starting at second ch from hook, sc 1, dc 1, tr 2, dc 1, sc 1**, rep from ** to ** 1 time, loosely ch 10), rep instructions in parentheses 1 more time; rep from * to * 2 times, ***loosely ch 17, and starting at second ch from hook, sc 1, dc 1, tr 2, dc 1, sc 1, rep from *** 1 more time.

Flowers

Make as many as you want and sew to vines and branch.

Using G hook and white yarn, *ch 4, hdc 1 in third ch from hook, sl st 1*, rep 5 times (5 petals). Sew petals together to form flower. Using yellow yarn and sewing in center of flowers, sew 2 flowers at double set of leaves on vine, and single flowers on branch.

Big Bird

Make 1.
Use blue yarn for bird.

Head

Rnd 1: Ch 2, 5 sc in second ch from hook.

Rnd 2: Sc 2 in each sc around. (10 sts)

Rnd 3: *Sc 1, 2 sc in next sc*, rep 5 times. (15 sts)

Rnd 4: *Sc 2, 2 sc in next sc*, rep 5 times. (20 sts)

Rnd 5: *Sc 3, 2 sc in next sc*, rep 5 times. (25 sts)

Rnd 6: *Sc 4, 2 sc in next sc*, rep 5 times. (30 sts)

Rnds 7–14: Sc 30.

Rnd 15: *Sc 4, dec 1*, rep 5 times. (25 sts)

Rnd 16: *Sc 3, dec 1*, rep 5 times. (20 sts)

Position and attach eyes, cut a bird beak from felt using the pattern on page 60, fold it in half, and sew to face.

Rnd 17: *Sc 2, dec 1*, rep 5 times. (15 sts)

Rnd 18: *Sc 1, dec 1*, rep 5 times. (10 sts)

Stuff head firmly.

Rnd 19: *Sk 1 sc, sc 1*, rep 5 times. (5 sts)

Fasten off, weave in end.

Body

Rnd 1: Ch 2, 5 sc in second ch from hook.

Rnd 2: Sc 2 in each sc around. (10 sts)

Rnd 3: *Sc 1, 2 sc in next sc*, rep 5 times. (15 sts)

Rnd 4: *Sc 2, 2 sc in next sc*, rep 5 times. (20 sts)

Rnd 5: *Sc 3, 2 sc in next sc*, rep 5 times. (25 sts)

Rnds 6–10: Sc 25.

Fasten off, leaving long tail for sewing. Stuff and sew to head.

Tail

Rnd 1: Sc 2, 6 sc in second ch from hook.

Rnd 2: Sc 2 in each sc around. (12 sts)

Rnds 3–9: Sc 12.

Fasten off, leaving long tail for sewing. Sew open end closed and sew to body.

Wings

Make 2.

Rnd 1: Ch 2, 5 sc in second ch from hook.

Rnd 2: Sc 2 in each sc around. (10 sts)

Rnds 3–7: Sc 10.

Fasten off, leaving long tail for sewing. Sew open end closed and sew to body.

Little Birds

Make 3.

Use blue yarn for all birds.

Head

Rnd 1: Ch 2, sc 5 in second ch from hook.

Rnd 2: Sc 2 in each sc around. (10 sts)

Rnd 3: *Sc 1, 2 sc in next sc*, rep 5 times. (15 sts)

Rnd 4: *Sc 2, 2 sc in next sc*, rep 5 times. (20 sts)

Rnd 5: *Sc 3, 2 sc in next sc*, rep 5 times. (25 sts)

Rnds 6–12: Sc 25.

Rnd 13: *Sc 3, dec 1*, rep 5 times. (20 sts)

Position and attach eyes, cut a bird beak from felt using the pattern on page 60, fold it in half, and sew to face.

Rnd 14: *Sc 2, dec 1*, rep 5 times. (15 sts)

Rnd 15: *Sc 1, dec 1*, rep 5 times. (10 sts)

Stuff head firmly.

Rnd 16: *Sk 1 sc, sc 1*, rep 5 times. (5 sts)

Fasten off and weave in end.

Body

Rnd 1: Ch 2, sc 5 in second ch from hook.

Rnd 2: Sc 2 in each sc around. (10 sts)

Rnd 3: *Sc 1, 2 sc in next sc*, rep 5 times. (15 sts)

Rnd 4: *Sc 2, 2 sc in next sc*, rep 5 times. (20 sts)

Rnds 5–8: Sc 20.

Fasten off, leaving long tail for sewing. Stuff and sew to head.

Tail

Rnd 1: Ch 2, sc 5 in second ch from hook.

Rnd 2: Sc 2 in each sc around. (10 sts)

Rnds 3–7: Sc 10.

Fasten off, leaving long tail for sewing. Sew open end closed and sew to body.

Wings

Make 2 for each bird.

Rnd 1: Ch 2, sc 8 in second ch from hook.

Rnds 2–5: Sc 8.

Fasten off, leaving long tail for sewing. Sew open end closed and sew to body.

Finishing the Mobile

Sew bottom leaf of vines to top of each bird's head.

Tie yellow yarn around ring, knot, insert G hook through ring, YO, bring hook toward you, and sc 1 to form loop around ring. Rep as many times as needed to cover ring.

Loosely ch 60, fasten off leaving long tail for sewing. Make 4 chains. Sew all four chains to ring. Sew other ends equal distance apart to branch.

Stitching → line

Bird beak

Hot-Air Balloon

When I was a little girl, I always thought it would be the best to fly in a hot-air balloon and see the beach and my house from up in the sky. This little bear is a lot luckier, though, because he hangs from the ceiling and gets to see my girls Oli and Martina when they're playing in their room.

Finished Size

Approx 12" from top of balloon to bottom of basket

Materials

Worsted-weight yarn in purple, yellow, orange, red, green, brown, and white
Size F-5 (3.75 mm) and G-6 (4 mm) crochet hooks
6 mm plastic eyes with safety backings
Black embroidery floss and tapestry needle
Fiberfill or stuffing of your choice

Balloon

Rnd 1: Using G and purple yarn, ch 2, 5 sc in second ch from hook.
Rnd 2: Sc 2 in each sc around. (10 sts)
Rnd 3: *Sc 1, 2 sc in next sc*, rep 5 times. (15 sts)
Rnd 4: Change to yellow yarn, *sc 2, 2 sc in next sc*, rep 5 times. (20 sts)
Rnd 5: *Sc 3, 2 sc in next sc*, rep 5 times. (25 sts)
Rnd 6: *Sc 4, 2 sc in next sc*, rep 5 times. (30 sts)

Rnd 7: Change to orange yarn, *sc 5, 2 sc in next sc*, rep 5 times. (35 sts)
Rnd 8: *Sc 6, 2 sc in next sc*, rep 5 times. (40 sts)
Rnd 9: *Sc 7, 2 sc in next sc*, rep 5 times. (45 sts)
Rnd 10: Using red yarn, *sc 8, 2 sc in next sc*, rep 5 times. (50 sts)
Rnd 11: *Sc 9, 2 sc in next sc*, rep 5 times. (55 sts)
Rnd 12: *Sc 10, 2 sc in next sc*, rep 5 times. (60 sts)
Rnds 13–15: Using green yarn, sc 60.
Rnds 16–18: Using purple yarn, sc 60.
Rnds 19–21: Using yellow yarn, sc 60.
Rnd 22: Using orange yarn, *sc 10, dec 1*, rep 5 times. (55 sts)
Rnd 23: Sc 55.
Rnd 24: *Sc 9, dec 1*, rep 5 times. (50 sts)
Rnd 25: Using red yarn, sc 50.
Rnd 26: *Sc 8, dec 1*, rep 5 times. (45 sts)
Rnd 27: Sc 45.
Rnd 28: Using green yarn, *sc 7, dec 1*, rep 5 times. (40 sts)
Rnd 29: Sc 40.
Rnd 30: *Sc 6, dec 1*, rep 5 times. (35 sts)

Rnd 31: Using purple yarn, sc 35.
Rnd 32: *Sc 5, dec 1*, rep 5 times. (30 sts)
Rnd 33: Sc 30.
Rnd 34: Using yellow yarn, *sc 4, dec 1*, rep 5 times. (25 sts)
Rnds 35 and 36: Sc 25.
Fasten off and weave in end.

Balloon Bottom

Rnd 1: Using orange yarn, ch 2, 5 sc in second ch from hook.
Rnd 2: Sc 2 in each sc around. (10 sts)
Rnd 3: *Sc 1, 2 sc in next sc*, rep 5 times. (15 sts)
Rnd 4: *Sc 2, 2 sc in next sc*, rep 5 times. (20 sts)
Rnd 5: *Sc 3, 2 sc in next sc*, rep 5 times. (25 sts)
Fasten off, leaving long tail for sewing. Stuff balloon almost to top and line up sts of circle with sts of open end of balloon, sew three-quarters of the way around, finish stuffing, and finish sewing. Weave in end.

Basket

Rnd 1: Using G hook and brown yarn, ch 2, 7 sc in second ch from hook.

Rnd 2: Sc 2 in each sc around. (14 sts)

Rnd 3: *Sc 1, 2 sc in next sc*, rep 7 times. (21 sts)

Rnd 4: *Sc 2, 2 sc in next sc*, rep 7 times. (28 sts)

Rnd 5: *Sc 3, 2 sc in next sc*, rep 7 times. (35 sts)

Rnds 6–12: Sc 35.

Fasten off and weave in end.

Bear

Use F hook and white yarn for bear.

Muzzle

Rnd 1: Ch 2, 5 sc in second ch from hook.

Rnd 2: Sc 2 in each sc around. (10 sts)

Rnd 3: *Sc 1, 2 sc in next sc*, rep 5 times. (15 sts)

Rnd 4: Sc 15.

Fasten off, leaving long tail for sewing. Embroider nose and mouth and set aside.

Head

Rnd 1: Ch 2, 6 sc in second ch from hook.

Rnd 2: Sc 2 in each sc around. (12 sts)

Rnd 3: *Sc 1, 2 sc in next sc*, rep 6 times. (18 sts)

Rnd 4: *Sc 2, 2 sc in next sc*, rep 6 times. (24 sts)

Rnd 5: *Sc 3, 2 sc in next sc*, rep 6 times. (30 sts)

Rnds 6–13: Sc 30.

Rnd 14: *Sc 3, dec 1*, rep 6 times. (24 sts)

Rnd 15: *Sc 2, dec 1*, rep 6 times. (18 sts)

Position and attach eyes, sew muzzle in place. Stuff head almost to top.

Rnd 16: *Sc 1, dec 1*, rep 6 times. (12 sts)

Rnd 17: Dec 6 times. (6 sts)

Fasten off and weave in end.

Ears

Make 2.

Ch 3, 6 hdc in third ch from hook.

Fasten off, leaving long tail for sewing. Sew to head and weave in ends.

Body

Rnd 1: Ch 2, 6 sc in second ch from hook.

Rnd 2: Sc 2 in each sc around. (12 sts)

Rnd 3: *Sc 1, 2 sc in next sc*, rep 6 times. (18 sts)

Rnds 4–7: Sc 18.

Fasten off, leaving long tail for sewing. Stuff and sew to head.

Arms and Legs

Make 2 of each.

Rnd 1: Ch 2, 6 sc in second ch from hook.

Rnds 2–6: Sc 6.

Fasten off, leaving long tail for sewing. Sew open end closed, sew to body, and weave in end.

Finishing

Cut 3 pieces of yarn (I used purple), each about 8" long. Sew pieces of yarn equidistant from each other around top of basket. Tie other ends of each piece of yarn to bottom circle of balloon, also equidistant from each other.

To hang balloon, cut a piece of yarn twice as long as you want the little balloon to hang. Fold yarn in half, insert folded end into sts at top of balloon, and pull ends through. Knot ends and hang it wherever you want!

Tuck little bear into basket.

These stroller toys would make a cute and original handmade present for a new baby. They're both colorful and fun to look at, and they're a great way to encourage talking about different colors and counting! They could also be hooked to a crib or car seat.

Finished Size

Approx 10" long from hanging loop to bottom of flower or fish

Materials

Worsted-weight yarn in green, yellow, white, orange, red, and blue

Size F-5 (3.75 mm) crochet hook

6 mm (for flowers) and 9 mm (for fish) plastic eyes with safety backings

Black embroidery floss and tapestry needle

Fiberfill or stuffing of your choice

1 pair of Velcro dots with sticky back for each toy

Stroller Ring and Stems

Using green yarn for garden flowers or blue yarn for fish, loosely ch 45.

Rnd 1: Sc 44, starting in second ch from hook.

Rnds 2 and 3: Ch 1, sc 44.

Fasten off and weave in end. Put a piece of Velcro on each end so that they face each other to close.

Long Stem

Make 1.

Loosely ch 51, sl st 50, starting at second ch from hook. Fasten off, leaving long tail for sewing.

Short Stem

Make 2.

Loosely ch 41, sl st 40, starting at second ch from hook. Fasten off, leaving long tail for sewing.

Sew end of stem around stroller ring, loose enough so that stem can move. You'll sew fish or flowers to other end.

Garden Flowers

Center

Make 3.

Rnd 1: Using yellow yarn, ch 2, 5 sc in second ch from hook.

Rnd 2: Sc 2 in each sc around. (10 sts)

Rnd 3: *Sc 1, 2 sc in next sc*, rep 5 times. (15 sts)

Rnd 4: *Sc 2, 2 sc in next sc*, rep 5 times. (20 sts)

Rnd 5: *Sc 3, 2 sc in next sc*, rep 5 times. (25 sts)

Position and attach eyes, embroider mouth.

Rnd 6: *Sc 4, 2 sc in next sc*, rep 5 times. (30 sts)

Rnds 7–12: Sc 30.

Rnd 13: *Sc 4, dec 1*, rep 5 times. (25 sts)

Rnd 14: *Sc 3, dec 1*, rep 5 times. (20 sts)

Rnd 15: *Sc 2, dec 1*, rep 5 times. (15 sts)

Rnd 16: *Sc 1, dec 1*, rep 5 times. (10 sts)

Rnd 17: *Sk 1 sc, sc 1*, rep 5 times. (5 sts)

Fasten off and weave in end.

Petals

Make 7 for each flower.

Rnd 1: Using red or white yarn, ch 2, 6 sc in second ch from hook.

Rnd 2: Sc 2 in each sc around. (12 sts)

Rnds 3–6: Sc 12.

Fasten off, leaving long tail for sewing. Sew open end closed.

Sew 7 petals to flower center. Sew 1 flower to end of each green stem.

Leaf

Make 3 total.

Rnd 1: Using green yarn, ch 2, 5 sc in second ch from hook.

Rnd 2: Sc 2 in each sc around. (10 sts)

Rnd 3: Sc 10.

Rnd 4: *Sc 1, 2 sc in next sc*, rep 5 times. (15 sts)

Rnd 5: Sc 15.

Rnd 6: *Sc 2, 2 sc in next sc*, rep 5 times. (20 sts)

Rnd 7: *Sc 2, dec 1*, rep 5 times. (15 sts)

Rnd 8: Sc 15.

Rnd 9: *Sc 1, dec 1*, rep 5 times. (10 sts)

Rnd 10: Sc 10.

Rnd 11: *Sk 1 sc, sc 1*, rep 5 times. (5 sts)

Fasten off, leaving long tail for sewing. Sew open end closed. Sew a leaf to each green stem as desired.

Fish in the Sea

Make 3.

Body

Rnd 1: Using desired yarn color, ch 2, 5 sc in second ch from hook.

Rnd 2: Sc 2 in each sc around. (10 sts)

Rnd 3: *Sc 1, 2 sc in next sc*, rep 5 times. (15 sts)

Rnd 4: Sc 15.

Rnd 5: *Sc 2, 2 sc in next sc*, rep 5 times. (20 sts)

Rnd 6: Sc 20.

Rnd 7: *Sc 3, 2 sc in next sc*, rep 5 times. (25 sts)

Position and attach eyes, embroider mouth.

Rnds 13–16: Sc 25.

Rnd 17: *Sc 3, dec 1*, rep 5 times. (20 sts)

Rnd 18: *Sc 2, dec 1*, rep 5 times. (15 sts)

Stuff almost to top.

Rnd 19: *Sc 1, dec 1*, rep 5 times.
(10 sts)
Finish stuffing.
Rnd 20: *Sk 1 sc, sc 1*, rep 5 times.
(5 sts)
Fasten off and weave in end.

Tail

Make 2 pieces for each tail; make 3 tails.
Rnd 1: Using color to match fish body,
ch 2, 5 sc in second ch from hook.
Rnd 2: Sc 2 in each sc around. (10 sts)
Rnds 3–7: Sc 10.
Rnd 8: Dec 5 times. (5 sts)
Rnd 9: Sc 5.
Fasten off, leaving long tail for sewing.
Sew 2 tail pieces next to each other
at end of body. Sew a fish to end of
each blue stem.

Algae

Make 3.
Loosely ch 52, and starting at third ch
from hook, dc 50, then loosely ch 57,
and starting in second ch from hook,
sc 56.
Fasten off, leaving long tail for sewing.
Fold where dc and sc meet and sew
this midpoint to blue chain that is
attached to stroller ring.

Finishing

Attach ring to stroller.

Every baby needs a rattle, and my girls' favorites were always the donut-shaped ones, probably because they were the easiest to hold. Why not make the baby in your life a couple of super-cute rattles?

Finished Size

Approx 3" diameter ring

Materials

Worsted-weight yarn in blue, green, orange, and red for rattles and tan, gray, white, black, yellow, and orange for animal heads

Size F-5 (3.75 mm) crochet hook

6 mm plastic eyes with safety backings

Small pieces of tan and white craft felt (for panda bear, bunny, and cat)

Sewing thread and sharp needle

Black, brown, and pink embroidery floss and tapestry needle

Fiberfill or stuffing of your choice

Jingle bells or rattle insert

Donut

Using desired yarn color, loosely ch 45.

Rnd 1: Join first and last sts with sl st to form a ring, being careful not to twist sts, and sc 45.

Rnds 2–11: Sc 45.

Fasten off, leaving long tail for sewing. Fold piece and sew edges together to form a donut shape, stuffing as you go.

Rattle Head

Rnd 1: Using brown (cat), white (panda), gray (bunny), or yellow (duck) yarn, ch 2, 5 sc in second ch from hook.

Rnd 2: Sc 2 in each sc around. (10 sts)

Rnd 3: *Sc 1, 2 sc in next sc*, rep 5 times. (15 sts)

Rnd 4: *Sc 2, 2 sc in next sc*, rep 5 times. (20 sts)

Rnd 5: *Sc 3, 2 sc in next sc*, rep 5 times. (25 sts)

Rnds 6–11: Sc 25.

Position and attach eyes. For cat, bunny, or panda, use the respective pattern on page 71 to cut a felt muzzle. Embroider nose and mouth and sew in place. For duck, sew on beak and wings (see page 71). Insert jingle bell or rattle.

Rnd 12: *Sc 3, dec 1*, rep 5 times. (20 sts)

Rnd 13: *Sc 2, dec 1*, rep 5 times. (15 sts)

Rnd 14: *Sc 1, dec 1*, rep 5 times. (10 sts)

Stuff firmly.

Rnd 15: *Sk 1 sc, sc 1*, rep 5 times. (5 sts)

Fasten off, leaving long tail for sewing. Sew to donut shape.

Panda and Bunny Ears

Make 2.

For panda:

Rnd 1: Using black yarn, ch 2, 6 sc in second ch from hook.

Rnd 2: Sc 6.

Fasten off, leaving long tail for sewing. Sew open end closed and sew to head.

For bunny:

Rnd 1: Using gray yarn, ch 2, 6 sc in second ch from hook.

Rnds 2–4: Sc 6.

Fasten off, leaving long tail for sewing. Sew open end closed and sew to head.

Cat Ears

Make 2.

Rnd 1: Using brown yarn, ch 2, 4 sc in second ch from hook.

Rnd 2: Sc 4.

Rnd 3: Sc 2 in each sc around. (8 sts)

Fasten off, leaving long tail for sewing. Sew open end closed and sew to head.

Duck Beak

Rnd 1: Using orange yarn, ch 2, sc 8 in second ch from hook.

Rnd 2: Sc 8.

Fasten off, leaving long tail for sewing. Sew to head.

Duck Wings

Make 2.

Rnd 1: Using yellow yarn, ch 2, sc 6 in second ch from hook.

Rnds 2 and 3: Sc 6.

Fasten off, leaving long tail for sewing. Sew open end closed and sew to body.

Creative Option

You could also use the rattle heads on wrist rattles. Just crochet a narrow rectangular piece, sew the rattle head to it, and join the ends with Velcro.

Panda muzzle

Bunny muzzle

Cat muzzle

Toys in Pajamas

I love kids in footed pajamas! The cutest pictures of our girls are of them wearing their footed pajamas, looking all sleepy and cuddly. What's could be cuter? Softies in pajamas, of course, with their very own little good-night toys.

Finished Sizes

Big Toys: Approx 9" tall
Little Toys: Approx 4" tall

Materials

Worsted-weight yarn in red, white, gray, pink, brown, and yellow

Size G-6 (4 mm) crochet hook

Plastic eyes with safety backings: 6 mm for little toys, 9 mm for bear and koala, 12 mm for bunnies

Small pieces of black, white, pink, and tan craft felt

Sewing thread and sharp needle

Black and pink embroidery floss and tapestry needle

Small decorative buttons for pajamas (optional)

Fiberfill or stuffing of your choice

Big Toys

The head, body, arms, and legs are the same for all the big toys. See page 75 for various style ears.

Head

Use white yarn for bunny, brown for bear, or gray for koala.

Rnd 1: Ch 2, 6 sc in second ch from hook.
Rnd 2: Sc 2 in each sc around. (12 sts)
Rnd 3: *Sc 1, 2 sc in next sc*, rep 6 times. (18 sts)
Rnd 4: *Sc 2, 2 sc in next sc*, rep 6 times. (24 sts)
Rnd 5: *Sc 3, 2 sc in next sc*, rep 6 times. (30 sts)
Rnd 6: *Sc 4, 2 sc in next sc*, rep 6 times. (36 sts)
Rnd 7: *Sc 5, 2 sc in next sc*, rep 6 times. (42 sts)
Rnd 8: *Sc 6, 2 sc in next sc*, rep 6 times. (48 sts)
Rnds 9–20: Sc 48.
Rnd 21: *Sc 6, dec 1*, rep 6 times. (42 sts)
Rnd 22: *Sc 5, dec 1*, rep 6 times. (36 sts)
Rnd 23: *Sc 4, dec 1*, rep 6 times. (30 sts)
Rnd 24: *Sc 3, dec 1*, rep 6 times. (24 sts)
Rnd 25: Sc 24.
For all, position and attach eyes (9 mm for bear and koala; 12 mm for bunny). For bunny or bear, use pattern on page 77 to cut a piece of white or tan felt for muzzle, embroider nose and mouth, and sew to face. For koala, use pattern on page 77 to cut a piece of black felt for nose, sew to face, and embroider mouth.
Rnd 26: *Sc 2, dec 1*, rep 6 times. (18 sts)
Rnd 27: Sc 18.
Stuff head firmly.
Rnd 28: *Sc 1, dec 1*, rep 6 times. (12 sts)
Rnd 29: *Sk 1 sc, sc 1*, rep 6 times. (6 sts)
Fasten off and weave in end.

Body

Use preferred yarn color for pajamas. If desired, work rnds 13–16 in white for stripe on koala pajamas.

Rnd 1: Ch 2, 6 sc in second ch from hook.
Rnd 2: Sc 2 in each sc around. (12 sts)
Rnd 3: *Sc 1, 2 sc in next sc*, rep 6 times. (18 sts)
Rnd 4: *Sc 2, 2 sc in next sc*, rep 6 times. (24 sts)
Rnd 5: *Sc 3, 2 sc in next sc*, rep 6 times. (30 sts)
Rnd 6: *Sc 4, 2 sc in next sc*, rep 6 times. (36 sts)
Rnds 7–14: Sc 36.
Rnd 15: *Sc 4, dec 1*, rep 6 times. (30 sts)
Rnds 16–21: Sc 30.
Fasten off, leaving long tail for sewing. Stuff body and sew to head. Sew two little buttons to pajamas if you wish—they look cute.

Hood for Bear

Rnd 1: Using yarn color to match pajamas, ch 2, 6 sc in second ch from hook.

Rnd 2: Sc 2 in each st around. (12 sts)

Rnd 3: *Sc 1, 2 sc in next sc*, rep 6 times. (18 sts)

Rnd 4: *Sc 2, 2 sc in next sc*, rep 6 times. (24 sts)

Rnd 5: *Sc 3, 2 sc in next sc*, rep 6 times. (30 sts)

Rnd 6: *Sc 4, 2 sc in next sc*, rep 6 times. (36 sts)

Rnd 7: *Sc 5, 2 sc in next sc*, rep 6 times. (42 sts)

Rnd 8: *Sc 6, 2 sc in next sc*, rep 6 times. (48 sts)

Rnds 9–20: Sc 48.

Fasten off, leaving long tail for sewing. Position hood on bear's head, making sure the back of hood touches the body (see photo below), sew to head and back of body (so it looks like it's a real hood).

Arms

Make 2.

Rnd 1: Using white, brown, or gray yarn to match animal, ch 2, 6 sc in second ch from hook.

Rnd 2: Sc 2 in each sc around. (12 sts)

Rnd 3: *Sc 1, 2 sc in next sc*, rep 6 times. (18 sts)

Rnds 4–6: Sc 18.

Rnd 7: *Sc 1, dec 1*, rep 6 times. (12 sts)

Rnd 8: Change to pajama color, sc 12.

Rnd 9: BPsc 12.

Rnds 10–21: Sc 12.

Fasten off, leaving long tail for sewing. Stuff, sew open end closed, and sew to body.

Legs

Make 2.

Rnd 1: Using yarn color to match pajamas, ch 2, 6 sc in second ch from hook.

Rnd 2: Sc 2 in each sc around. (12 sts)

Rnd 3: *Sc 1, 2 sc in next sc*, rep 6 times. (18 sts)

Rnd 4: *Sc 2, 2 sc in next sc*, rep 6 times. (24 sts)

Rnd 5: Sc 24.

Rnd 6: Dc 6, sc 18.

Rnd 7: Hdc 6, sc 18.

Rnd 8: *Sc 2, dec 1*, rep 6 times. (18 sts)

Rnd 9: *Sc 1, dec 1*, rep 6 times. (12 sts)

Rnds 10–18: Sc 12.

Fasten off, leaving long tail for sewing. Stuff and sew to body.

Bear Ears

Make 2.

Rnd 1: Using brown yarn, ch 2, 6 sc in second ch from hook.

Rnd 2: Sc 2 in each sc around. (12 sts)

Rnd 3: *Sc 1, 2 sc in next sc*, rep 6 times. (18 sts)

Rnds 4–7: Sc 18.

Fasten off, leaving long tail for sewing. Sew open end closed and sew ears to hood.

Bunny Ears

Make 2.

Using white yarn, loosely ch 30.

Rnd 1: Hdc 28 starting in third bump at back of chain (see "Working in Chain Loops," page 171), and then work 28 hdc on opposite side of chain (front loops of chain). (56 sts)

Rnd 2: *Hdc 4 in first sc, hdc 27, rep from * once.

Fasten off, leaving long tail for sewing. Using pattern on page 77, cut 2 big bunny ears from white felt and sew to ear. Sew ears to head.

Koala Ears

Make 2.

Rnd 1: Using gray yarn, ch 2, 6 sc in second ch from hook.

Rnd 2: Sc 2 in each sc around. (12 sts)

Rnd 3: *Sc 1, 2 sc in next sc*, rep 6 times. (18 sts)

Rnd 4: *Sc 2, 2 sc in next sc*, rep 6 times. (24 sts)

Rnds 5–8: Sc 24.

Fasten off, leaving long tail for sewing. Sew open end closed and sew ears to head.

Little Toys

Use white yarn for bunny, brown for bear, or gray for koala.

Head

Rnd 1: Ch 2, 6 sc in second ch from hook.

Rnd 2: Sc 2 in each sc around. (12 sts)

Rnd 3: *Sc 1, 2 sc in next sc*, rep
6 times. (18 sts)

Rnd 4: *Sc 2, 2 sc in next sc*, rep
6 times. (24 sts)

Rnd 5: *Sc 3, 2 sc in next sc*, rep
6 times. (30 sts)

Rnds 6–13: Sc 30.

Rnd 14: *Sc 3, dec 1*, rep 6 times.
(24 sts)

Position and attach eyes: For bear, use
pattern on page 77 to cut 2 tan felt
eyes. Place felt and insert 6 mm eyes
through felt and head. For koala,
use 9 mm eyes and use 12 mm eyes
for bunny. Use patterns on page 77
to cut muzzle or nose from felt: For
bunny or bear, cut a piece of white
or tan felt, embroider nose and
mouth, and sew to face. For koala,
cut a piece of black felt for nose, sew
to face, and embroider mouth.

Rnd 15: *Sc 2, dec 1*, rep 6 times.
(18 sts)

Rnd 16: *Sc 1, dec 1*, rep 6 times.
(12 sts)

Stuff firmly.

Rnd 17: *Sk 1 st, sc 1*, rep 6 times.
(6 sts)

Fasten off and weave in end.

Body

Rnd 1: Ch 2, 6 sc in second ch from
hook.

Rnd 2: Sc 2 in each sc around. (12 sts)

Rnd 3: *Sc 1, 2 sc in next sc*, rep
6 times. (18 sts)

Rnds 4–7: Sc 18.

Fasten off, leaving long tail for sewing.
Stuff and sew body to head.

Arms and Legs

Make 2 of each.

Rnd 1: Ch 2, 6 sc in second ch from
hook.

Rnds 2–5: Sc 6.

Fasten off, leaving long tail for sewing.
Sew open end closed and sew to
body.

Bunny Ears

Make 2.

Loosely ch 15. Hdc 12 starting in
third bump at back of chain (see
page 171), and then work 12 hdc on
opposite side of chain (front loops of
chain). (24 sts)

Fasten off, leaving long tail for sewing.
Using little bunny ear pattern on
page 77, cut and sew pink felt to
ears. Sew ears to head.

Koala Ears

Make 2.

Rnd 1: Ch 2, 5 sc in second ch from
hook.

Rnd 2: Sc 2 in each sc around. (10 sts)

Rnd 3: *Sc 1, sc 2 in next sc*, rep
5 times. (15 sts)

Rnds 4–6: Sc 15.

Fasten off, leaving long tail for sewing.
Sew open end closed and sew
to head.

Bear Ears

Make 2.

Rnd 1: Ch 2, 6 sc in second ch from
hook.

Rnd 2: Sc 2 in each sc around. (12 sts)

Rnds 3 and 4: Sc 12.

Fasten off, leaving long tail for sewing.
Sew open end closed and sew
to head.

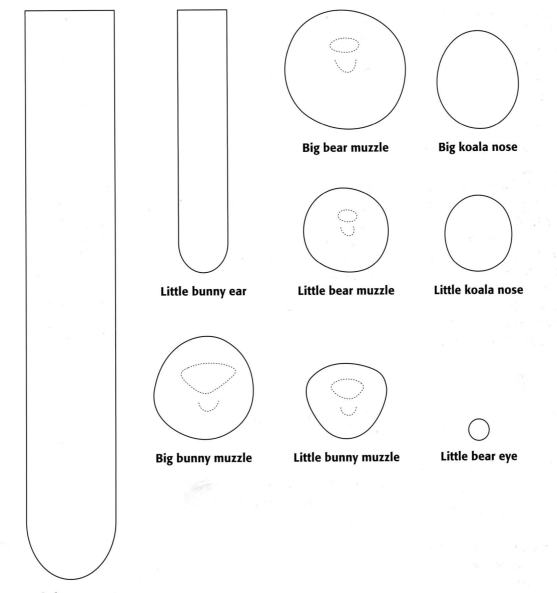

Big bear muzzle

Big koala nose

Little bunny ear

Little bear muzzle

Little koala nose

Big bunny muzzle

Little bunny muzzle

Little bear eye

Big bunny ear

Tool Set

When I gave these tools to Martina for "quality control," she kissed the hammer, asked "him" if he was sleepy, and put him to bed! I ended up making her a set without the eyes, and she's been fixing everything around our house. Decide if you want the eyes or not and make a tool set for your favorite girl or boy.

Finished Sizes

Screwdriver: Approx 6½" long
File: Approx 7" long
Pliers: Approx 6" long
Hammer: Approx 7½" long

Materials

Worsted-weight yarn in orange, green, and gray

Size F-5 (3.75 mm) crochet hook

Plastic eyes with safety backings: 6 mm for screwdriver and file, 9 mm for hammer

Black embroidery floss and tapestry needle

Fiberfill or stuffing of your choice

Screwdriver and File

Handle

Make 1 for each tool.

Rnd 1: Using orange yarn, ch 2, 7 sc in second ch from hook.

Rnd 2: Sc 2 in each sc around. (14 sts)

Rnds 3–7: Sc 14.

Position and attach 6 mm eyes; embroider mouth.

Rnds 8–20: Sc 14, stuffing as you go.

Rnd 21: Sc 14 through back loops only.

Rnd 22: Dec 7 times. (7 sts)

Sl st 1, fasten off, leaving long tail. Insert tail into tapestry needle and weave through rem 7 sts to close hole, weave in end.

Screwdriver

Using gray yarn, loosely ch 7.

Rnd 1: Sc 6 starting in second bump at back of chain (see "Working in Chain Loops," page 171), and then work 6 sc on opposite side of chain (front loops of chain). (12 sts)

Rnds 2–4: Sc 12.

Rnd 5: *Sc 1, dec 1*, rep 4 times. (8 sts)

Rnds 6–18: Sc 8, stuffing as you go.

Sl st 1, fasten off, leaving long tail for sewing. Sew to handle.

File

Using gray yarn, loosely ch 7.

Rnd 1: Sc 6 starting in second bump at back of chain (see page 171), and then work 6 sc on opposite side of chain (front loops of chain). (12 sts)

Rnds 2–20: Sc 12.

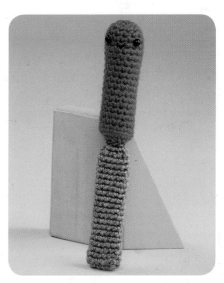

Rnd 21: *Sc 1, dec 1*, rep 4 times. (8 sts)
Rnd 22: Sc 8.
Fasten off, leaving long tail for sewing.
   Sew to handle.

Hammer

Handle

Rnd 1: Using green yarn, ch 2, 8 sc in
   second ch from hook.
Rnd 2: Sc 2 in each sc around. (16 sts)
Rnd 3: *Sc 1, 2 sc in next sc*, rep
   8 times. (24 sts)
Rnd 4: Through back loops only, *sc 1,
   dec 1*, rep 8 times. (16 sts)
Rnds 5–35: Sc 16, stuffing as you go.
Rnd 36: Change to gray, sc 16 through
   back loops only.
Rnds 37–43: Sc 16.

Position and attach 9 mm eyes;
   embroider mouth.
Rnd 44: Sc 16 through back loops only.
Rnd 45: Dec 8 times. (8 sts)
Sl st 1, fasten off, leaving long tail to
   close 8-st hole, weave in end.

Hammer Head

Rnd 1: Using gray yarn, ch 2, 8 sc in
   second chain from hook.
Rnd 2: Sc 2 in each sc around. (16 sts)
Rnd 3: *Sc 1, 2 sc in next sc*, rep
   8 times. (24 sts)
Rnd 4: Through back loops only, *sc 1,
   dec 1*, rep 8 times. (16 sts)
Rnds 5–7: Sc 16.
Rnd 8: Sc 16 through back loops only.
   Stuff.
Rnd 9: Dec 8 times. (8 sts)
Rnd 10: Sc 8 through front loops only.
Rnd 11: Sc 8.
Sl st 1, fasten off, leaving long tail for
   sewing. Finish stuffing and sew to
   gray portion of hammer handle.

Hammer Claw

Make 2.
Rnd 1: Using gray yarn, ch 2, 3 sc in
   second ch from hook.
Rnd 2: Sc 3.
Rnd 3: Sc 2 in each sc around. (6 sts)
Rnds 4–7: Sc 6.
Sl st 1, fasten off, leaving long tail for
   sewing. Sew 2 pieces next to each
   hammer handle, opposite of the
   hammer head.

Pliers

Make 2.
Rnd 1: Using green yarn, ch 2, 6 sc in
   second ch from hook.
Rnd 2: Sc 2 in each sc around. (12 sts)
Rnds 3–18: Sc 12, stuffing as you go.
Rnd 19: *Sc 1, dec 1*, rep 4 times. (8 sts)
Rnds 20 and 21: Sc 8.
Finish stuffing and change to gray yarn.
   No more stuffing after this!
Rnd 22: Sc 8 through back loops only.
Rnds 23–33: Sc 8.
Rnd 34: Dec 4 times. (4 sts)
Fasten off and weave in end. Position
   1 piece on top of the other and sew
   together just above green handles.
   Shape the pliers so they look like the
   real thing.

I made this baby for Oli right before Martina was born and gave it to her when we got home from the hospital with Marti. Every time I'd change Martina's diaper, Oli would change her baby's diaper, and it was the cutest thing to watch.

Finished Size

Approx 9½" tall

Materials

Worsted-weight yarn in desired skin color, and white for diaper and beanie

Size G-6 (4 mm) and 7 (4.5 mm) crochet hooks; use G hook unless otherwise instructed

9 mm plastic eyes with safety backings

Brown and red embroidery floss and tapestry needle

Fiberfill or stuffing of your choice

2 pieces of Velcro with sticky back for diaper

Baby

Use skin-colored yarn throughout.

Head

Rnd 1: Ch 2, 6 sc in second ch from hook.

Rnd 2: Sc 2 in each sc around. (12 sts)

Rnd 3: *Sc 1, 2 sc in next sc*, rep 6 times. (18 sts)

Rnd 4: *Sc 2, 2 sc in next sc*, rep 6 times. (24 sts)

Rnd 5: *Sc 3, 2 sc in next sc*, rep 6 times. (30 sts)

Rnd 6: *Sc 4, 2 sc in next sc*, rep 6 times. (36 sts)

Rnd 7: *Sc 5, 2 sc in next sc*, rep 6 times. (42 sts)

Rnds 8–19: Sc 42.

Rnd 20: *Sc 5, dec 1*, rep 6 times. (36 sts)

Rnd 21: *Sc 4, dec 1*, rep 6 times. (30 sts)

Rnd 22: *Sc 3, dec 1*, rep 6 times. (24 sts)

Position and attach eyes; embroider mouth and nose.

Rnd 23: Sc 24.

Rnd 24: *Sc 2, dec 1*, rep 6 times. (18 sts)

Rnd 25: *Sc 1, dec 1*, rep 6 times. (12 sts)

Stuff head.

Rnd 26: *Sk 1 sc, sc 1*, rep 6 times. (6 sts)

Fasten off and weave in end.

Body

Rnd 1: Ch 2, 6 sc in second ch from hook.

Rnd 2: Sc 2 in each sc around. (12 sts)

Rnd 3: *Sc 1, 2 sc in next sc*, rep 6 times. (18 sts)

Rnd 4: *Sc 2, 2 sc in next sc*, rep 6 times. (24 sts)

Rnd 5: *Sc 3, 2 sc in next sc*, rep 6 times. (30 sts)

Rnd 6: *Sc 4, 2 sc in next sc*, rep 6 times. (36 sts)

Rnds 7–14: Sc 36.

Rnd 15: *Sc 4, dec 1*, rep 6 times. (30 sts)

Rnds 16 and 17: Sc 30.

Rnd 18: *Sc 3, dec 1*, rep 6 times. (24 sts)

Rnds 19 and 20: Sc 24.

Fasten off, leaving long tail for sewing. Stuff and sew body to head.

Arms

Make 2.

Rnd 1: Ch 2, 6 sc in second ch from hook.

Rnd 2: Sc 2 in each sc around. (12 sts)

Rnds 3–23: Sc 12, stuffing as you go.

Fasten off, leaving long tail for sewing. Sew open end closed and sew to body.

Legs

Make 2.

Rnd 1: Ch 2, 6 sc in second ch from hook.

Rnd 2: Sc 2 in each sc around. (12 sts)

Rnd 3: *Sc 1, 2 sc in next sc*, rep 6 times. (18 sts)

Rnd 4: *Sc 2, 2 sc in next sc*, rep 6 times. (24 sts)

Rnds 5 and 6: Hdc 12, sc 12.

Rnd 7: *Sc 2, dec 1*, rep 6 times. (18 sts)

Rnd 8: *Sc 1, dec 1*, rep 6 times. (12 sts)

Rnds 9–20: Sc 12, stuffing as you go.

Fasten off, leaving long tail for sewing. Sew to body.

Diaper

The diaper is worked back and forth in rows. Using white yarn, loosely ch 31.

Row 1: Sc 30, starting in second ch from hook, turn.

Rows 2–7: Ch 1, sc 30, turn.

Row 8: Sl st 10, sc 10, turn.

Row 9: Ch 1, sc 10, turn.

Row 10: Sk 1 sc, sc 7, sk 1 sc, sc 1, turn. (8 sts)

Row 11: Sk 1 sc, sc 5, sk 1 sc, sc 1, turn. (6 sts)

Row 12: Sk 1 sc, sc 3, sk 1 sc, sc 1, turn. (4 sts)

Rows 13–16: Ch 1, sc 4, turn.

Row 17: Ch 1, 2 sc in first sc, sc 2, 2 sc in last sc, turn. (6 sts)

Row 18: Ch 1, 2 sc in first sc, sc 4, 2 sc in last sc, turn. (8 sts)

Row 19: Ch 1, 2 sc in first sc, sc 6, 2 sc in last sc, turn. (10 sts)

Row 20: Ch 1, 2 sc in first sc, sc 8, 2 sc in last sc, turn. (12 sts)

Row 21: Ch 1, 2 sc in first sc, sc 10, 2 sc in last sc, turn. (14 sts)

Row 22: Ch 1, 2 sc in first sc, sc 12, 2 sc in last sc, turn. (16 sts)

Rows 23–26: Ch 1, sc 16, turn.

Fasten off and weave in end.

Attach Velcro pieces on WS at each end of longer piece and on RS at each end of shorter piece (see photo above).

Hat

Rnd 1: Using white yarn and a size 7 hook, ch 2, 6 sc in second ch from hook.

Rnd 2: Sc 2 in each sc around. (12 sts)

Rnd 3: *Sc 1, 2 sc in next sc*, rep 6 times. (18 sts)

Rnd 4: *Sc 2, 2 sc in next sc*, rep 6 times. (24 sts)

Rnd 5: *Sc 3, 2 sc in next sc*, rep 6 times. (30 sts)

Rnd 6: *Sc 4, 2 sc in next sc*, rep 6 times. (36 sts)

Rnd 7: *Sc 5, 2 sc in next sc*, rep 6 times. (42 sts)

Rnds 8–16: Sc 42.

Fasten off and weave in end.

Little Turtles, Eggs, and Their Mommy

With this toy turtle, kids can count the eggs in mommy turtle's "belly" and count the baby turtles that are born. Best of all, the eggs and babies can be stored inside the mommy turtle, so they won't be lost under a bed or couch.

Finished Sizes

Mommy turtle: Approx 3" tall x 7" long
Little turtles: Approx 1½" tall
Eggs: Approx 2" tall

Materials

Worsted-weight yarn in green, brown, orange, and white
Size G-6 (4 mm) crochet hook
Plastic eyes with safety backings: 9 mm for mommy and 2 sets of 6 mm for babies
Tapestry needle
Fiberfill or stuffing of your choice

Mommy Turtle

Shell Top

Rnd 1: Using brown yarn, ch 2, 6 sc in second ch from hook.
Rnd 2: Sc 2 in each sc around. (12 sts)
Rnd 3: *Sc 1, 2 sc in next sc*, rep 6 times. (18 sts)
Rnd 4: *Sc 2, 2 sc in next sc*, rep 6 times. (24 sts)
Rnd 5: *Sc 3, 2 sc in next sc*, rep 6 times. (30 sts)
Rnd 6: *Sc 4, 2 sc in next sc*, rep 6 times. (36 sts)

Rnd 7: *Sc 5, 2 sc in next sc*, rep 6 times. (42 sts)
Rnd 8: *Sc 6, 2 sc in next sc*, rep 6 times. (48 sts)
Rnd 9: *Sc 7, 2 sc in next sc*, rep 6 times. (54 sts)
Rnd 10: *Sc 8, 2 sc in next sc*, rep 6 times. (60 sts)
Rnd 11: *Sc 9, 2 sc in next sc*, rep 6 times. (66 sts)
Rnd 12: *Sc 10, 2 sc in next sc*, rep 6 times. (72 sts)
Rnds 13–23: Sc 72.
Rnd 24: Sc 72 through back loops only.
Fasten off and weave in ends.
To create segments on the shell, using orange yarn, backstitch embroider 3 rings around the shell, working the first 1 between the 7th and 8th row from the center at the top of the shell. Embroider the second ring 7 rows from the first line, and the third ring 7 rows from the second one. Then divide the rings into 4 equal segments and embroider a vertical line between the rings at each division, offsetting the lines between circles as shown.

C   A   B

Backstitch

Shell Bottom

Rnd 1: Using orange yarn, ch 2, 6 sc in second ch from hook.
Rnd 2: Sc 2 in each sc around. (12 sts)
Rnd 3: *Sc 1, 2 sc in next sc*, rep 6 times. (18 sts)
Rnd 4: *Sc 2, 2 sc in next sc*, rep 6 times. (24 sts)
Rnd 5: *Sc 3, 2 sc in next sc*, rep 6 times. (30 sts)
Rnd 6: *Sc 4, 2 sc in next sc*, rep 6 times. (36 sts)
Rnd 7: *Sc 5, 2 sc in next sc*, rep 6 times. (42 sts)
Rnd 8: *Sc 6, 2 sc in next sc*, rep 6 times. (48 sts)
Rnd 9: *Sc 7, 2 sc in next sc*, rep 6 times. (54 sts)

Rnd 10: *Sc 8, 2 sc in next sc*, rep 6 times. (60 sts)

Rnd 11: *Sc 9, 2 sc in next sc*, rep 6 times. (66 sts)

Rnd 12: *Sc 10, 2 sc in next sc*, rep 6 times. (72 sts)

Rnds 13 and 14: Sc 72.

Fasten off and weave in end.

Head

Rnd 1: Using green yarn, ch 2, 5 sc in second ch from hook.

Rnd 2: Sc 2 in each sc around. (10 sts)

Rnd 3: *Sc 1, 2 sc in next sc*, rep 5 times. (15 sts)

Rnd 4: *Sc 2, 2 sc in next sc*, rep 5 times. (20 sts)

Rnd 5: Sc 20.

Rnd 6: *Sc 3, 2 sc in next sc*, rep 5 times. (25 sts)

Rnds 7–11: Sc 25.

Position and attach 9 mm eyes.

Rnd 12: *Sc 3, dec 1*, rep 5 times. (20 sts)

Rnds 13–19: Sc 20.

Fasten off, leaving long tail for sewing. Stuff firmly, sew open end closed, and sew to shell bottom. (Make sure right side of shell is facing down when you sew head and legs.)

Front Legs

Make 2.

Rnd 1: Using green yarn, ch 2, 5 sc in second ch from hook.

Rnd 2: Sc 2 in each sc around. (10 sts)

Rnd 3: Sc 10.

Rnd 4: *Sc 1, 2 sc in next sc*, rep 5 times. (15 sts)

Rnds 5–12: Sc 15.

Rnds 13–15: Hdc 8 in front loops only, sc 7.

Rnds 16–19: Sc 15.

Fasten off, leaving long tail for sewing. Stuff lightly, sew open end closed, and sew to shell bottom.

Back Legs

Make 2.

Rnd 1: Using green yarn, ch 2, 5 sc in second ch from hook.

Rnd 2: Sc 2 in each sc around. (10 sts)

Rnd 3: Sc 10.

Rnd 4: *Sc 1, 2 sc in next sc*, rep 5 times. (15 sts)

Rnds 5–15: Sc 15.

Fasten off, leaving long tail for sewing. Stuff lightly, sew open end closed, and sew to shell bottom.

Finishing

Align sts of shell top with sts of shell bottom and sew tog, leaving an opening between back legs big enough to fit one of the eggs (see photo, below left).

Join brown yarn to 1 of front sts you left in rnd 24 of shell top.

Rnd 1: Sc 72.

Rnds 2 and 3: Hdc 72.

Fasten off and weave in end.

Little Turtle

Make 2.

Shell Top

Rnd 1: Using brown yarn, ch 2, 6 sc in second ch from hook.

Rnd 2: Sc 2 in each sc around. (12 sts)

Rnd 3: *Sc 1, 2 sc in next sc*, rep 6 times. (18 sts)

Rnds 4–6: Sc 18.

Rnd 7: Sc 18 through back loops only.

Fasten off and weave in end.

Shell Bottom

Rnd 1: Using brown yarn, ch 2, 6 sc in second ch from hook.

Rnd 2: Sc 2 in each sc around. (12 sts)

Rnd 3: *Sc 1, 2 sc in next sc*, rep 6 times. (18 sts)

Fasten off, leaving long tail for sewing.

Head

Rnd 1: Using green yarn, ch 2, 5 sc in second ch from hook.

Rnd 2: Sc 2 in each sc around. (10 sts)

Rnd 3: *Sc 1, 2 sc in next sc*, rep 5 times. (15 sts)

Rnds 4 and 5: Sc 15.

Position and attach 6 mm eyes.

Rnd 6: *Sc 1, dec 1*, rep 5 times. (10 sts)

Fasten off, leaving long tail for sewing. Stuff head and sew to shell top, above rnd 7.

Legs

Make 4.

Rnd 1: Using green yarn, ch 2, 5 sc in second ch from hook.

Rnds 2–4: Sc 5.

Fasten off, leaving long tail for sewing. Sew open end closed and sew to shell bottom.

Finishing

Align sts of shell top with sts of shell bottom and sew around.

Join brown yarn to 1 of front sts you left in rnd 7 of shell top.

Rnd 1: Sc 18.

Rnd 2: Sc 18.

Fasten off and weave in end.

Whole Egg

Make 4.

Rnd 1: Using white yarn, ch 2, 5 sc in second ch from hook.

Rnd 2: Sc 2 in each sc around. (10 sts)

Rnd 3: *Sc 1, 2 sc in next sc*, rep 5 times. (15 sts)

Rnd 4: *Sc 2, 2 sc in next sc*, rep 5 times. (20 sts)

Rnd 5: *Sc 3, 2 sc in next sc*, rep 5 times. (25 sts)

Rnds 6–12: Sc 25.

Rnd 13: *Sc 3, dec 1*, rep 5 times. (20 sts)

Rnd 14: *Sc 2, dec 1*, rep 5 times. (15 sts)

Stuff lightly.

Rnd 15: *Sc 1, dec 1*, rep 5 times. (10 sts)

Rnd 16: *Sk 1 sc, sc 1*, rep 5 times. (5 sts)

Fasten off and weave in ends.

Cracked Egg

Make 1.

Rnd 1: Using white yarn, ch 2, 5 sc in second ch from hook.

Rnd 2: Sc 2 in each sc around. (10 sts)

Rnd 3: *Sc 1, 2 sc in next sc*, rep 5 times. (15 sts)

Rnd 4: *Sc 2, 2 sc in next sc*, rep 5 times. (20 sts)

Rnd 5: *Sc 3, 2 sc in next sc*, rep 5 times. (25 sts)

Rnds 6–10: Sc 25.

Rnd 11: * Sl st 1, hdc 2, dc 2*, rep 4 more times.

Fasten off and weave in ends.

Little Fish and Her Daddy

Martina has always liked fish. As a tiny newborn, she would stare at my computer screen saver, full of colorful fishes swimming around, and now she loves to go to the pet store and spend time with her head stuck to the huge fish tanks! Make a huge school of colorful fishes for your favorite fish lover and let them pretend to swim together.

Finished Sizes

Daddy fish: Approx 7" long
Little fish: Approx 5" long

Materials

Worsted-weight yarn in blue, green, red, and orange
Size G-6 (4 mm) crochet hook
2 sets of 9 mm plastic eyes with safety backings
Black embroidery floss and tapestry needle
Fiberfill or stuffing of your choice

Daddy Fish

Make 1.

Eye Roundies

Make 2.
Rnd 1: Using blue yarn, ch 2, 6 sc in second ch from hook.
Rnd 2: Sc 2 in each sc around. (12 sts)
Fasten off, leaving long tail for sewing, set aside.

Body

Rnd 1: Using green yarn, ch 2, 6 sc in second ch from hook.
Rnd 2: Sc 2 in each sc around. (12 sts)
Rnd 3: Sc 12.
Rnd 4: *Sc 1, 2 sc in next sc*, rep 6 times. (18 sts)
Rnd 5: Sc 18.
Rnd 6: *Sc 2, 2 sc in next sc*, rep 6 times. (24 sts)
Rnd 7: Sc 24.
Rnd 8: *Sc 3, 2 sc in next sc*, rep 6 times. (30 sts)
Rnd 9: Sc 30.
Rnd 10: *Sc 4, 2 sc in next sc*, rep 6 times. (36 sts)
Rnds 11–13: Sc 36.
Insert plastic eyes through eye roundies, attach eyes to head, sew roundies to head, and embroider mouth.
Change to blue yarn and alternate 1 rnd blue and 1 rnd green to end of body.
Rnds 14–24: Sc 36.
Rnd 25: *Sc 4, dec 1*, rep 6 times. (30 sts)
Rnd 26: *Sc 3, dec 1*, rep 6 times. (24 sts)
Rnd 27: *Sc 2, dec 1*, rep 6 times. (18 sts)
Rnd 28: Sc 18.
Stuff almost to top.

Rnd 29: *Sc 1, dec 1*, rep 6 times. (12 sts)
Rnd 30: Sc 12.
Finish stuffing.
Rnd 31: *Sk 1 sc, sc 1*, rep 6 times. (6 sts)
Fasten off and weave in end.

Top Fin

Rnd 1: Using blue yarn, ch 2, 8 sc in second ch from hook.
Rnd 2: Sc 2 in each sc around. (16 sts)
Rnds 3–5: Sc 16.
Fasten off, leaving long tail for sewing. Sew to top of body.

Side Fin

Make 2.
Rnd 1: Using blue yarn, ch 2, 6 sc in second ch from hook.
Rnd 2: Sc 2 in each sc around. (12 sts)
Rnd 3: *Sc 1, 2 sc in next sc*, rep 6 times. (18 sts)
Rnds 4–6: Sc 18.
Rnd 7: *Sc 1, dec 1*, rep 6 times. (12 sts)
Rnd 8: *Sk 1 sc, sc 1*, rep 6 times. (6 sts)
Rnds 9 and 10: Sc 6.
Fasten off, leaving long tail for sewing. Sew to side of body.

Tail

Make 2.

Rnd 1: Using blue yarn, ch 2, 6 sc in second ch from hook.

Rnd 2: Sc 6.

Rnd 3: Sc 2 in each sc around. (12 sts)

Rnd 4: Sc 12.

Rnd 5: *Sc 1, 2 sc in next sc*, rep 6 times. (18 sts)

Rnd 6: Sc 18.

Rnd 7: *Sc 2, 2 sc in next sc*, rep 6 times. (24 sts)

Rnds 8–12: Sc 24.

Rnd 13: *Sc 2, dec 1*, rep 6 times. (18 sts)

Rnd 14: Sc 18.

Rnd 15: *Sc 1, dec 1*, rep 6 times. (12 sts)

Rnd 16: Sc 12.

Rnd 17: *Sk 1 sc, sc 1*, rep 6 times. (6 sts)

Fasten off, leaving long tail for sewing. Sew 2 tails next to each other at end of body.

Bottom Fin

Rnd 1: Using blue yarn, ch 2, 5 sc in second ch from hook.

Rnd 2: Sc 2 in each sc around. (10 sts)

Rnds 3 and 4: Sc 10.

Fasten off, leaving long tail for sewing, and sew to bottom of fish.

Little Fish

Make 1.

Eye Roundies

Make 2.

Rnd 1: Using red yarn, ch 2, 6 sc in second ch from hook.

Rnd 2: Sc 2 in each sc around. (12 sts)

Fasten off, leaving long tail for sewing, set aside.

Body

Rnd 1: Using orange yarn, ch 2, 6 sc in second ch from hook.

Rnd 2: Sc 2 in each sc around. (12 sts)

Rnd 3: Sc 12.

Rnd 4: *Sc 1, 2 sc in next sc*, rep 6 times. (18 sts)

Rnd 5: Sc 18.

Rnd 6: *Sc 2, 2 sc in next sc*, rep 6 times. (24 sts)

Rnds 7–11: Sc 24.

Insert plastic eyes through eye roundies, attach eyes to head, sew roundies to head, and embroider mouth.

Change to red yarn and alternate 1 rnd red and 1 rnd orange to end of body.

Rnds 12–16: Sc 24.

Rnd 17: *Sc 2, dec 1*, rep 6 times. (18 sts)

Rnd 18: Sc 18.

Stuff almost to top.

Rnd 19: *Sc 1, dec 1*, rep 6 times. (12 sts)

Rnd 20: Sc 12.

Finish stuffing.

Rnd 21: *Sk 1 sc, sc 1*, rep 6 times. (6 sts)

Fasten off and weave in end.

Top Fin

Rnd 1: Using red yarn, ch 2, 6 sc in second ch from hook.

Rnd 2: Sc 2 in each sc around. (12 sts)

Rnds 3 and 4: Sc 12.

Fasten off, leaving long tail for sewing. Sew to top of body.

Side Fin

Make 2.

Rnd 1: Using red yarn, ch 2, 6 sc in second ch from hook.

Rnd 2: Sc 2 in each sc around. (12 sts)

Rnds 3–6: Sc 12.

Rnd 7: *Sk 1 sc, sc 1*, rep 6 times. (6 sts)

Rnd 8: Sc 6.

Fasten off, leaving long tail for sewing. Sew to side of body.

Tail

Make 2.

Rnd 1: Using red yarn, ch 2, 6 sc in second ch from hook.

Rnd 2: Sc 6.

Rnd 3: Sc 2 in each sc around. (12 sts)

Rnd 4: Sc 12.

Rnd 5: *Sc 1, 2 sc in next sc*, rep 6 times. (18 sts)

Rnds 6–8: Sc 18.

Rnd 9: *Sc 1, dec 1*, rep 6 times. (12 sts)

Rnd 10: Sc 12.

Rnd 11: Sk 1 sc, sc 1. (6 sts)

Fasten off, leaving long tail for sewing. Sew 2 tails next to each other at end of body.

Bottom Fin

Rnd 1: Using red yarn, ch 2, 6 sc in second ch from hook.

Rnds 2 and 3: Sc 6.

Fasten off, leaving long tail for sewing, and sew to bottom of body.

Finishing

Weave in all ends.

Little Squirrel and Her Mommy

When I was pregnant with Oli, I had a nightmare about squirrels trying to attack me. I've been terrified of squirrels ever since. Oli thinks it's the funniest story and loves to tell it to random people. You should see their faces—they probably think I'm nuts! I made these squirrels to get over my phobia, and while it didn't work, I think you'll like them!

Finished Sizes

Mommy squirrel: Approx 5½" tall
Little squirrel: Approx 4½" tall

Materials

Worsted-weight yarn in tan, brown, red, and white
Size G-6 (4 mm) crochet hook
12 mm brown plastic eyes with safety backings
Small pieces of tan and white craft felt
Sewing thread and sharp needle
Brown embroidery floss and tapestry needle
Fiberfill or stuffing of your choice

Mommy Squirrel

Use tan yarn for head, body, ears, and arms.

Head

Rnd 1: Ch 2, 6 sc in second ch from hook.
Rnd 2: Sc 2 in each sc around. (12 sts)
Rnd 3: *Sc 1, 2 sc in next sc*, rep 6 times. (18 sts)
Rnd 4: *Sc 2, 2 sc in next sc*, rep 6 times. (24 sts)
Rnd 5: *Sc 3, 2 sc in next sc*, rep 6 times. (30 sts)
Rnd 6: *Sc 4, 2 sc in next sc*, rep 6 times. (36 sts)
Rnds 7–17: Sc 36.
Rnd 18: *Sc 4, dec 1*, rep 6 times. (30 sts)
Rnd 19: *Sc 3, dec 1*, rep 6 times. (24 sts)
Position and attach eyes. Using pattern on page 94, cut a piece of tan felt, embroider mouth and nose, and sew it to head.
Rnd 20: *Sc 2, dec 1*, rep 6 times. (18 sts)
Stuff firmly.
Rnd 21: *Sc 1, dec 1*, rep 6 times. (12 sts)
Finish stuffing.
Rnd 22: *Sk 1 sc, sc 1*, rep 6 times. (6 sts)
Fasten off and weave in ends.

Ears

Make 2.
Rnd 1: Ch 2, 5 sc in second ch from hook.
Rnd 2: Sc 5.
Rnd 3: Sc 2 in each sc around. (10 sts)
Rnds 4 and 5: Sc 10.
Fasten off, leaving long tail for sewing. Sew to head.

Body

Rnd 1: Ch 2, 6 sc in second ch from hook.
Rnd 2: Sc 2 sc in each sc around. (12 sts)
Rnd 3: *Sc 1, 2 sc in next sc*, rep 6 times. (18 sts)
Rnd 4: *Sc 2, 2 sc in next sc*, rep 6 times. (24 sts)
Rnds 5–13: Sc 24.
Fasten off, leaving long tail for sewing. Stuff and sew to head.

Arms

Make 2.
Rnd 1: Ch 2, 5 sc in second ch from hook.
Rnd 2: Sc 2 sc in each sc around. (10 sts)

Rnds 3–8: Sc 10.

Fasten off, leaving long tail for sewing. Sew open end closed and sew to body. (I didn't stuff them.)

Legs

Make 2.

Rnd 1: Using brown yarn, ch 2, 5 sc in second ch from hook.

Rnd 2: Sc 2 in each sc around. (10 sts)

Rnds 3–11: Sc 10.

Fasten off, leaving long tail for sewing. Stuff, sew open end tog and set aside.

Tail

Rnd 1: Using brown yarn, ch 2, 6 sc in second ch from hook.

Rnd 2: Sc 2 in each sc around. (12 sts)

Rnd 3: *Sc 1, 2 sc in next sc*, rep 6 times. (18 sts)

Rnd 4: *Sc 2, 2 sc in next sc*, rep 6 times. (24 sts)

Rnd 5: *Sc 3, 2 sc in next sc*, rep 6 times. (30 sts)

Rnds 6–13: Sc 30.

Rnd 14: *Sc 3, dec 1*, rep 6 times. (24 sts)

Rnds 15–21: Sc 24.

Rnd 22: *Sc 2, dec 1*, rep 6 times. (18 sts)

Rnds 23–32: Sc 18.

Fasten off, leaving long tail for sewing. Stuff lightly near the top, sew open end closed, and sew bottom of tail between legs as shown above right. Then sew bottom of tail/leg unit to bottom of body around inside of legs and tail. Sew top of tail to back of head to keep tail upright.

Sew bottom of tail between legs.

Sew legs and tail to body.

Mushroom

Make 1.

Top

Rnd 1: Using red yarn, ch 2, 6 sc in second ch from hook.

Rnd 2: Sc 2 in each sc around. (12 sts)

Rnd 3: *Sc 1, 2 sc in next sc*, rep 6 times. (18 sts)

Rnd 4: *Sc 2, 2 sc in next sc*, rep 6 times. (24 sts)

Rnds 5–9: Sc 24.

Rnd 10: *Sc 2, dec 1*, rep 6 times. (18 sts)

Using pattern on page 94, cut a white felt dot and sew to mushroom.

Rnd 11: *Sc 1, dec 1*, rep 6 times. (12 sts)

Stuff.

Rnd 12: *Sk 1 sc, sc 1*, rep 6 times. (6 sts)

Fasten off and weave in end.

Stem

Rnd 1: Using white yarn, ch 2, 6 sc in second ch from hook.

Rnd 2: Sc 2 in each sc around. (12 sts)

Rnd 3: Sc 12.

Fasten off, leaving long tail for sewing. Stuff and sew to top of mushroom. Sew mushroom between mommy squirrel's arms.

Little Squirrel

Make 1. Use tan yarn for head, ears, body and arms.

Head

Rnd 1: Ch 2, 6 sc in second ch from hook.

Rnd 2: Sc 2 in each sc around. (12 sts)

Rnd 3: *Sc 1, 2 sc in next sc*, rep 6 times. (18 sts)

Rnd 4: *Sc 2, 2 sc in next sc*, rep 6 times. (24 sts)

Rnd 5: *Sc 3, 2 sc in next sc*, rep 6 times. (30 sts)

Rnds 6–14: Sc 30.

Rnd 15: *Sc 3, dec 1*, rep 6 times. (24 sts)

Position and attach eyes. Using pattern, right, cut a muzzle from tan felt, embroider mouth and nose, and sew it to face.

Rnd 16: *Sc 2, dec 1*, rep 6 times. (18 sts)

Rnd 17: *Sc 1, dec 1*, rep 6 times. (12 sts)

Stuff.

Rnd 18: *Sk 1 sc, sc 1*, rep 6 times. (6 sts)

Fasten off and weave in end.

Ears

Make 2.

Rnd 1: Ch 2, 5 sc in second ch from hook.

Rnd 2: Sc 5.

Rnd 3: Sc 2 in each sc around. (10 sts)

Fasten off, leaving long tail for sewing. Sew to head.

Body

Rnd 1: Ch 2, 6 sc in second ch from hook.

Rnd 2: Sc 2 in each sc around. (12 sts)

Rnd 3: *Sc 1, 2 sc in next sc*, rep 6 times. (18 sts)

Rnds 4–12: Sc 18.

Fasten off, leaving long tail for sewing. Stuff and sew to head.

Arms

Make 2.

Rnd 1: Ch 2, 6 sc in second ch from hook.

Rnds 2–5: Sc 6.

Fasten off, leaving long tail for sewing. Sew open end closed and sew to body.

Tail

Rnd 1: Using brown yarn, ch 2, 6 sc in second ch from hook.

Rnd 2: Sc 2 in each sc around. (12 sts)

Rnd 3: *Sc 1, 2 sc in next sc*, rep 6 times. (18 sts)

Rnds 4–16: Sc 18.

Rnd 17: *Sc 1, dec 1*, rep 6 times. (12 sts)

Rnds 18 and 19: Sc 12.

Fasten off, leaving long tail for sewing. Stuff tail lightly, sew open end closed, and sew to body. Weave in ends.

Legs

Make 2.

Rnd 1: Using brown yarn, ch 2, 6 sc in second ch from hook.

Rnds 2–8: Sc 6.

Fasten off, leaving long tail for sewing. Sew open end closed and sew to body. Weave in ends.

Mommy squirrel muzzle

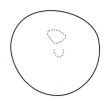

Little squirrel muzzle

Mushroom dot

Little Tiger and Her Mommy

When Oli was little, her favorite book was *I Don't Want to Go to Bed!* by Julie Sykes and Tim Warnes, a story of a little tiger that doesn't want to go to sleep. So for a while she wanted tiger everything—tiger shirts, tiger books, and tiger toys! Here is my version of a little tiger and her mom. Hope your little tiger likes it too.

Finished Sizes

Mommy tiger: Approx 9" tall
Little tiger: Approx 7" tall

Materials

Worsted-weight yarn in orange, black, and white
Size G-6 (4 mm) crochet hook
9 mm plastic eyes with safety backings
Black embroidery floss and tapestry needle
Fiberfill or stuffing of your choice

Mommy Tiger

Make 1.

Muzzle

Rnd 1: Using white yarn, ch 2, 6 sc in second ch from hook.
Rnd 2: Sc 2 in each sc around. (12 sts)
Rnd 3: *Sc 1, 2 sc in next sc*, rep 6 times. (18 sts)
Rnds 4 and 5: Sc 18.
Fasten off, leaving long tail for sewing. Embroider nose and mouth; set aside.

Head

Rnd 1: Using orange yarn, ch 2, 6 sc in second ch from hook.
Rnd 2: Sc 2 in each sc around. (12 sts)
Rnd 3: *Sc 1, 2 sc in next sc*, rep 6 times. (18 sts)
Rnd 4: *Sc 2, 2 sc in next sc*, rep 6 times. (24 sts)
Rnd 5: *Sc 3, 2 sc in next sc*, rep 6 times. (30 sts)
Rnd 6: *Sc 4, 2 sc in next sc*, rep 6 times. (36 sts)
Rnd 7: *Sc 5, 2 sc in next sc*, rep 6 times. (42 sts)
Rnds 8–19: Sc 42.
Rnd 20: *Sc 5, dec 1*, rep 6 times. (36 sts)
Rnd 21: *Sc 4, dec 1*, rep 6 times. (30 sts)
Rnd 22: *Sc 3, dec 1*, rep 6 times. (24 sts)
Position and attach eyes. Sew muzzle in place.
Rnd 23: *Sc 2, dec 1*, rep 6 times. (18 sts)
Rnd 24: Sc 18.
Stuff head firmly.
Rnd 25: *Sc 1, dec 1*, rep 6 times. (12 sts)
Fasten off and weave in end.

Ears

Make 2.
Rnd 1: Using orange yarn, ch 2, 6 sc in second ch from hook.
Rnd 2: Sc 6.
Rnd 3: Sc 2 in each sc around. (12 sts)
Rnd 4: Sc 12.
Fasten off, leaving long tail for sewing. Sew to head.

Head Stripes

Use black yarn for all stripes.

Stripes A (Top of Head)
Make 2.
Loosely ch 13. Beg at second ch from hook, sl st 1, sc 2, hdc 2, dc 2, hdc 2, sc 2, sl st 1.
Fasten off, leaving long tail for sewing. Sew to top of head.

Stripe B (Back of Head)
Loosely ch 16. Beg at second ch from hook, sl st 1, sc 2, hdc 2, dc 5, hdc 2, sc 2, sl st 1.
Fasten off, leaving long tail for sewing. Sew at back of head below A stripes.

Loosely ch 19. Beg at second ch from
hook, sl st 1, sc 2, hdc 2, dc 8, hdc 2,
sc 2, sl st 1.

Fasten off, leaving long tail for sewing.
Sew at back of head below B stripe.

Stripes on Cheeks

Make 4.

Loosely ch 9. Beg at second ch from
hook, sl st 1, sc 2, hdc 2, sc 2, sl st 1.

Fasten off, leaving long tail for sewing.
Sew to face.

Body

Rnd 1: Using orange yarn, ch 2, 6 sc in
second ch from hook.

Rnd 2: Sc 2 in each sc around. (12 sts)

Rnd 3: *Sc 1, 2 sc in next sc*, rep
6 times. (18 sts)

Rnd 4: *Sc 2, 2 sc in next sc*, rep
6 times. (24 sts)

Rnd 5: *Sc 3, 2 sc in next sc*, rep
6 times. (30 sts)

Rnd 6: *Sc 4, 2 sc in next sc*, rep
6 times. (36 sts)

Rnds 7–14: Sc 36.

Rnd 15: *Sc 4, dec 1*, rep 6 times.
(30 sts)

Rnds 16–19: Sc 30.

Fasten off, leaving long tail for sewing.
Stuff firmly and sew to head.

Body Stripes

Make 3.

Using black yarn, loosely ch 33. Beg at
second ch from hook: Sl st 1, sc 2,
hdc 2, dc 22, hdc 2, sc 2, sl st 1.

Fasten off, leaving long tail for sewing.
Sew around body.

Legs and Arms

Make 4.

Rnd 1: Using orange yarn, ch 2, 7 sc in
second ch from hook.

Rnd 2: Sc 2 in each sc around. (14 sts)

Rnds 3–15: Sc 14.

Fasten off, leaving long tail for sewing.
Stuff, sew open ends of arms closed,
and sew to body; sew legs to body.

Tail

Rnd 1: Using orange yarn, ch 2, 6 sc in
second ch from hook.

Rnd 2: Sc 6.

Rep rnd 2 until tail is approx 4" long.

Fasten off, leaving tail for sewing. Sew
open end closed and sew to body.

Little Tiger

Make 1.

Muzzle

Rnd 1: Using white yarn, ch 2, 6 sc in
second ch from hook.

Rnd 2: Sc 2 in each sc around. (12 sts)

Rnds 3 and 4: Sc 12.

Fasten off, leaving long tail for sewing.
Embroider nose and mouth, set
aside.

Head

Rnd 1: Using orange yarn, ch 2, 6 sc in
second ch from hook.

Rnd 2: Sc 2 in each sc around. (12 sts)

Rnd 3: *Sc 1, 2 sc in next sc*, rep 6 times. (18 sts)

Rnd 4: *Sc 2, 2 sc in next sc*, rep 6 times. (24 sts)

Rnd 5: *Sc 3, 2 sc in next sc*, rep 6 times. (30 sts)

Rnd 6: *Sc 4, 2 sc in next sc*, rep 6 times. (36 sts)

Rnds 7–17: Sc 36.

Rnd 18: *Sc 4, dec 1*, rep 6 times. (30 sts)

Rnd 19: *Sc 3, dec 1*, rep 6 times. (24 sts)

Position and attach eyes. Sew muzzle in place.

Rnd 20: *Sc 2, dec 1*, rep 6 times. (18 sts)

Rnd 21: Sc 18.

Rnd 22: *Sc 1, dec 1*, rep 6 times. (12 sts)

Stuff head firmly.

Rnd 23: *Sk 1 sc, sc 1*, rep 6 times. (6 sts)

Fasten off and weave in ends.

Ears

Make 2.

Rnd 1: Using orange yarn, ch 2, 6 sc in second ch from hook.

Rnd 2: Sc 6.

Rnd 3: Sc 2 in each sc around. (12 sts)

Rnd 4: Sc 12.

Fasten off, leaving long tail for sewing. Sew to head.

Head Stripes

Use black yarn for all stripes.

Stripes A (Top of Head)

Make 2.

Loosely ch 10. Beg at second ch from hook, sl st 1, sc 2, hdc 3, sc 2, sl st 1.

Fasten off, leaving long tail for sewing. Sew stripes to top of head.

Stripes B (Back of Head)

Make 2.

Loosely ch 15. Beg at second ch from hook, sl st 1, sc 2, hdc 8, sc 2, sl st 1.

Fasten off, leaving long tail for sewing. Sew stripes to back of head below A stripes.

Stripes on Cheeks

Make 2.

Loosely ch 9. Beg at second ch from hook, sl st 1, sc 2, hdc 2, sc 2, sl st 1.

Fasten off, leaving long tail for sewing. Sew stripes to face.

Body

Rnd 1: Using orange yarn, ch 2, 6 sc in second ch from hook.

Rnd 2: Sc 2 in each sc around. (12 sts)

Rnd 3: *Sc 1, 2 sc in next sc*, rep 6 times. (18 sts)

Rnd 4: *Sc 2, 2 sc in next sc*, rep 6 times. (24 sts)

Rnd 5: *Sc 3, 2 sc in next sc*, rep 6 times. (30 sts)

Rnds 6–12: Sc 30.

Rnd 13: *Sc 3, dec 1*, rep 6 times. (24 sts)

Rnds 14–16: Sc 24.

Fasten off, leaving long tail for sewing. Stuff firmly and sew to head.

Body Stripes

Make 2.

Using black yarn, loosely ch 29. Beg at second ch from hook, sl st 1, sc 2, hdc 22, sc 2, sl st 1.

Fasten off, leaving long tail for sewing. Sew stripes around body.

Legs and Arms

Make 4.

Rnd 1: Using orange yarn, ch 2, 6 sc in second ch from hook.

Rnd 2: Sc 2 in each sc around. (12 sts)

Rnds 3–12: Sc 12.

Fasten off, leaving long tail for sewing. Stuff, sew open end closed, and sew to body.

Tail

Rnd 1: Using orange yarn, ch 2, 4 sc in second ch from hook.

Rnd 2: Sc 4.

Rep rnd 2 until tail is approx 3" long.

Fasten off, leaving a tail for sewing. Sew open end closed and sew to body.

Little Bee and Her Mommy

After seeing *Bee Movie*, I just had to make some bees. Make a few more baby bees and hang them from the Branch Mobile (page 56) or use them in a Stroller Toy (page 65). They'll look really cute!

Finished Sizes

Mommy bee: Approx 5½" tall
Little bee: Approx 4" tall

Materials

Worsted-weight yarn in white, yellow, and black
Size G-6 (4 mm) crochet hook
9 mm plastic eyes with safety backings
Black embroidery floss and tapestry needle
Fiberfill or stuffing of your choice

Mommy Bee

Head

Rnd 1: Using black yarn, ch 2, sc 6 in second ch from hook.
Rnd 2: Sc 2 in each sc around. (12 sts)
Rnd 3: *Sc 1, 2 sc in next sc*, rep 6 times. (18 sts)
Rnd 4: *Sc 2, 2 sc in next sc*, rep 6 times. (24 sts)
Rnd 5: *Sc 3, 2 sc in next sc*, rep 6 times. (30 sts)
Rnd 6: *Sc 4, 2 sc in next sc*, rep 6 times. (36 sts)
Rnds 7 and 8: Sc 36.
Rnds 9–15: Using yellow yarn, sc 36.

Rnd 16: *Sc 4, dec 1*, rep 6 times. (30 sts)
Rnd 17: Sc 30.
Position and attach eyes. Embroider mouth.
Rnd 18: *Sc 3, dec 1*, rep 6 times. (24 sts)
Rnd 19: *Sc 2, dec 1*, rep 6 times. (18 sts)
Rnd 20: *Sc 1, dec 1*, rep 6 times. (12 sts)
Stuff head.
Rnd 21: *Sk 1 sc, sc 1*, rep 6 times. (6 sts)
Fasten off and weave in ends.

Body

Starting with black yarn, alternate 1 rnd yellow and 1 rnd black to end of body.
Rnd 1: Ch 2, sc 6 in second ch from hook.
Rnd 2: Sc 6.
Rnd 3: Sc 2 in each sc around. (12 sts)
Rnd 4: Sc 12.
Rnd 5: *Sc 1, 2 sc in next sc*, rep 6 times. (18 sts)
Rnd 6: Sc 18.
Rnd 7: *Sc 2, 2 sc in next sc*, rep 6 times. (24 sts)
Rnds 8–15: Sc 24.
Fasten off, leaving long tail for sewing. Stuff and sew to head.

Wings

Make 4.
Rnd 1: Using white yarn, ch 2, sc 6 in second ch from hook.
Rnd 2: Sc 2 in each sc around. (12 sts)
Rnds 3–9: Sc 12.
Rnd 10: Dec 6 times. (6 sts)
Rnd 11: Sc 6.
Fasten off, leaving long tail for sewing. Sew open end closed and sew 2 wings to each side of body.
See "Finishing" below to add antenna.

Finishing

Join black yarn to side of head in first row of black above yellow. Ch 6, fasten off, and weave in end. Rep on other side.

Little Bee

Head

Rnd 1: Using black yarn, ch 2, sc 6 in second ch from hook.
Rnd 2: Sc 2 in each sc around. (12 sts)
Rnd 3: *Sc 1, 2 sc in next sc*, rep 6 times. (18 sts)
Rnd 4: *Sc 2, 2 sc in next sc*, rep 6 times. (24 sts)
Rnd 5: *Sc 3, 2 sc in next sc*, rep 6 times. (30 sts)

Rnds 6 and 7: Sc 30.

Rnds 8–13: Using yellow yarn, sc 30.

Rnd 14: *Sc 3, dec 1*, rep 6 times. (24 sts)

Rnd 15: Sc 24.

Position and attach eyes. Embroider mouth.

Rnd 16: *Sc 2, dec 1*, rep 6 times. (18 sts)

Rnd 17: *Sc 1, dec 1*, rep 6 times. (12 sts)

Stuff head.

Rnd 18: *Sk 1 sc, sc 1*, rep 6 times. (6 sts)

Fasten off and weave in end.

Body

Starting with black yarn, alternate 1 rnd yellow and 1 rnd black to end of body.

Rnd 1: Ch 2, sc 6 in second ch from hook.

Rnd 2: Sc 6.

Rnd 3: Sc 2 in each sc around. (12 sts)

Rnd 4: Sc 12.

Rnd 5: *Sc 1, 2 sc in next sc*, rep 6 times. (18 sts)

Rnds 6–11: Sc 18.

Fasten off, leaving long tail for sewing. Stuff and sew to head.

Wings

Make 4.

Rnd 1: Using white yarn, ch 2, sc 5 in second ch from hook.

Rnd 2: Sc 2 in each sc around. (10 sts)

Rnds 3–6: Sc 10.

Rnd 7: Dec 5 times. (5 sts)

Rnd 8: Sc 5.

Fasten off, leaving long tail for sewing. Sew open end closed on each wing and sew 2 wings to each side of body.

Finishing

Join black yarn to side of head in first row of black above yellow. Ch 4, fasten off, and weave in end. Rep on other side.

Boy and Girl Robots

Once in a while Oli and Martina like to pretend they're robots. The funniest part is the talking—even they think it's funny and giggle like crazy while asking for cookies and trying to walk as if they're covered in cement! This is a really easy pattern, and you could customize it and add more "lights" here and there and even some shiny sequins to make your kid's favorite little robot.

Finished Sizes

Boy: Approx 8" tall
Girl: Approx 8" tall

Materials

Worsted-weight yarn in gray, blue, green, yellow, pink, red, and white
Size G-6 (4 mm) crochet hook
15 mm plastic eyes with safety backings
Black and red embroidery floss and tapestry needle
Fiberfill or stuffing of your choice

Body

Rnd 1: Using gray yarn, ch 2, 5 sc in second ch from hook.
Rnd 2: Sc 2 in each sc around. (10 sts)
Rnd 3: *Sc 1, 2 sc in next sc*, rep 5 times. (15 sts)
Rnd 4: *Sc 2, 2 sc in next sc*, rep 5 times. (20 sts)
Rnd 5: *Sc 3, 2 sc in next sc*, rep 5 times. (25 sts)
Rnd 6: *Sc 4, 2 sc in next sc*, rep 5 times. (30 sts)

Rnd 7: *Sc 5, 2 sc in next sc*, rep 5 times. (35 sts)
Rnd 8: *Sc 6, 2 sc in next sc*, rep 5 times. (40 sts)
Rnds 9–17: Sc 40.
Position and attach eyes. Embroider mouth.
Rnds 18–20: Using green yarn for boy or pink yarn for girl, sc 40.
Rnds 21–25: Using blue yarn for boy or red yarn for girl, sc 40.
Rnds 26–28: Change to green or pink and sc 40.
Rnd 29: Change to blue or red and sc 40 through back loops only.
Rnd 30: *Sc 6, dec 1*, rep 5 times. (35 sts)
Rnd 31: *Sc 5, dec 1*, rep 5 times. (30 sts)
Rnd 32: *Sc 4, dec 1*, rep 5 times. (25 sts)
Stuff almost to top.
Rnd 33: *Sc 3, dec 1*, rep 5 times. (20 sts)
Rnd 34: *Sc 2, dec 1*, rep 5 times. (15 sts)
Finish stuffing.

Rnd 35: *Sc 1, dec 1*, rep 5 times. (10 sts)
Rnd 36: Dec 5 times. (5 sts)
Fasten off, leaving long tail to close up the little hole.

Antenna

Make 1 for boy, 2 for girl.

Stem

Rnd 1: Using gray yarn, ch 2, sc 4 in second ch from hook.
Rnds 2–4: Sc 4.
Fasten off, leaving long tail for sewing, set aside.

Light

Rnd 1: Using yellow or white yarn, ch 2, 6 sc in second ch from hook.
Rnd 2: Sc 2 in each sc around. (12 sts)
Rnds 3–6: Sc 12.
Stuff.
Rnd 7: Dec 6 times. (6 sts)
Fasten off, leaving long tail for sewing. Sew light to end of stem. Sew 1 antenna to top of boy's head. Sew 2 antennae to sides of girl's head.

Arms

Make 2 lights and 2 arms.

Light at Top of Arm

Rnd 1: Using yellow or white yarn, ch 2, 5 sc in second ch from hook.

Rnd 2: Sc 2 in each sc around. (10 sts)

Rnd 3: *Sc 1, 2 sc in next sc*, rep 5 times. (15 sts)

Rnds 4–7: Sc 15.

Fasten off, leaving long tail for sewing. Stuff and sew to body.

Arms

Rnd 1: Using gray yarn, ch 2, 5 sc in second ch from hook.

Rnd 2: Sc 2 in each sc around. (10 sts)

Rnds 3–9: Sc 10, stuffing as you go.

Fasten off, leaving long tail for sewing. Stuff and sew to lights.

Legs

Make 2. Start at bottom of leg and use blue yarn for boy or red yarn for girl.

Rnd 1: Ch 2, 5 sc in second ch from hook.

Rnd 2: Sc 2 in each sc around. (10 sts)

Rnd 3: *Sc 1, 2 sc in next sc*, rep 5 times. (15 sts)

Rnd 4: *Sc 2, 2 sc in next sc*, rep 5 times. (20 sts)

Rnd 5: Through back loops only, *sc 2, dec 1*, rep 5 times. (15 sts)

Rnd 6: Sc 15 through back loops only.

Rnd 7: Change to green for boy or pink for girl and sc 15 through back loops only.

Rnd 8: Sc 15.

Rnd 9: Change to gray yarn and sc 15 through back loops only.

Rnd 10: *Sc 1, dec 1*, rep 5 times. (10 sts)

Rnds 11–13: Sc 10.

Fasten off, leaving a long tail for sewing. Sew to body.

The thing with little kids and balls in my house is that the balls always end up under the couch—or they disappear completely! I was thinking of making some kind of container to hold the balls, and it occurred to me that it would be adorable to have sweet pea balls—and here they are, in their own pod container! My kids love to play with their vegetables.

Finished Sizes

Peapod: Approx 4" wide x 10" long
Peas: Approx 3" in diameter

Materials

Worsted-weight yarn in pink and two
  shades of green
Size F-5 (3.75 mm), G-6 (4 mm), and H-8
  (5 mm) crochet hooks
9 mm plastic eyes with safety backings
Small piece of pink craft felt
Sewing thread and sharp needle
Black embroidery floss and tapestry
  needle
Fiberfill or stuffing of your choice

Peapod

Using G hook and darker shade of
  green yarn, ch 51.
Rnd 1: Sc 50 starting in second bump
  at back of chain (see "Working in
  Chain Loops," page 171), then work
  50 sc on opposite side of chain (front
  loops of chain). (100 sts)
Rnds 2–22: Sc 100.
Rnd 23: Switch to F hook and sc 100.
Fasten off and weave in ends.

Peas

Make 3. Use G hook and lighter shade
  of green yarn.
Rnd 1: Ch 2, 6 sc in second ch from
  hook.
Rnd 2: Sc 2 in each sc around. (12 sts)
Rnd 3: *Sc 1, 2 sc in next sc*, rep
  6 times. (18 sts)
Rnd 4: *Sc 2, 2 sc in next sc*, rep
  6 times. (24 sts)
Rnd 5: *Sc 3, 2 sc in next sc*, rep
  6 times. (30 sts)
Rnd 6: *Sc 4, 2 sc in next sc*, rep
  6 times. (36 sts)
Rnd 7: *Sc 5, 2 sc in next sc*, rep
  6 times. (42 sts)
Rnds 8–18: Sc 42.
Rnd 19: *Sc 5, dec 1*, rep 6 times.
  (36 sts)
Rnd 20: *Sc 4, dec 1*, rep 6 times.
  (30 sts)
Position and attach eyes. Embroider
  mouth. Using pattern, below right,
  cut 2 cheeks from felt and sew to
  head.
Rnd 21: *Sc 3, dec 1*, rep 6 times. (24 sts)
Rnd 22: *Sc 2, dec 1*, rep 6 times. (18 sts)
Stuff pea.

Rnd 23: *Sc 1, dec 1*, rep 6 times.
  (12 sts)
Rnd 24: Dec 6 times. (6 sts)
Fasten off, leaving long tail to close up
  hole, and weave in end.

Hat

Rnd 1: Using H hook and pink yarn,
  ch 2, 6 sc in second ch from hook.
Rnd 2: Sc 2 in each sc around. (12 sts)
Rnd 3: *Sc 1, 2 sc in next sc*, rep
  6 times. (18 sts)
Rnd 4: *Sc 2, 2 sc in next sc*, rep
  6 times. (24 sts)
Rnd 5: *Sc 3, 2 sc in next sc*, rep
  6 times. (30 sts)
Rnd 6: *Sc 4, 2 sc in next sc*, rep
  6 times. (36 sts)
Rnd 7: *Sc 5, 2 sc in next sc*, rep
  6 times. (42 sts)
Rnds 8–15: Sc 42.
Fasten off and weave in ends.

Sweet pea cheek

I've written this pattern for three different sizes of mushrooms, but once you make them all, it will be easy to figure out how to make them in other sizes since the pattern increases evenly. Apart from making wonderful little friends and pincushions, they can be used as sorting toys for little kids!

Finished Sizes

Small: Approx 2¾" tall
Medium: Approx 3" tall
Large: Approx 3½" tall

Materials

Worsted-weight yarn in red and white
Size E-4 (3.5 mm) and F-5 (3.75) crochet hooks
6 mm plastic eyes with safety backings
Small pieces of white craft felt
Sewing thread and sharp needle
Black embroidery floss and tapestry needle
Fiberfill or stuffing of your choice

Small Mushroom

Cap

Rnd 1: Using F hook and red yarn, ch 2, 6 sc in second ch from hook.
Rnd 2: Sc 2 in each sc around. (12 sts)
Rnd 3: *Sc 1, 2 sc in next sc*, rep 6 times. (18 sts)
Rnd 4: *Sc 2, 2 sc in next sc*, rep 6 times. (24 sts)
Rnd 5: *Sc 3, 2 sc in next sc*, rep 6 times. (30 sts)
Rnd 6: *Sc 4, 2 sc in next sc*, rep 6 times. (36 sts)
Rnds 7–12: Sc 36.
Rnd 13: *Sc 4, dec 1*, rep 6 times. (30 sts)
Rnd 14: *Sc 3, dec 1*, rep 6 times. (24 sts)
Using pattern on page 109, cut 3 small mushroom spots of white felt and sew to mushroom cap.
Rnd 15: *Sc 2, dec 1*, rep 6 times. (18 sts)
Rnd 16: *Sc 1, dec 1*, rep 6 times. (12 sts)
Stuff.
Rnd 17: Dec 6 times, sl st 1. (6 sts)
Fasten off and weave in ends.

Stem

Rnd 1: Using E hook and white yarn, ch 2, 5 sc in second ch from hook.
Rnd 2: Sc 2 in each sc around. (10 sts)
Rnd 3: *Sc 1, 2 sc in next sc*, rep 5 times. (15 sts)
Rnd 4: *Sc 2, 2 sc in next sc*, rep 5 times. (20 sts)
Rnd 5: *Sc 3, 2 sc in next sc*, rep 5 times. (25 sts)

Rnd 6: Through back loops only, *sc 3, dec 1*, rep 5 times. (20 sts)
Rnds 7–11: Sc 20.
Fasten off, leaving long tail for sewing.
Position and attach eyes. Embroider mouth.
Stuff and sew stem to cap.

Medium Mushroom

Cap

Rnd 1: Using F hook and red yarn, ch 2, 6 sc in second ch from hook.
Rnd 2: Sc 2 in each sc around. (12 sts)
Rnd 3: *Sc 1, 2 sc in next sc*, rep 6 times. (18 sts)
Rnd 4: *Sc 2, 2 sc in next sc*, rep 6 times. (24 sts)
Rnd 5: *Sc 3, 2 sc in next sc*, rep 6 times. (30 sts)
Rnd 6: *Sc 4, 2 sc in next sc*, rep 6 times. (36 sts)
Rnd 7: *Sc 5, 2 sc in next sc*, rep 6 times. (42 sts)
Rnds 8–14: Sc 42.
Rnd 15: *Sc 5, dec 1*, rep 6 times. (36 sts)
Rnd 16: *Sc 4, dec 1*, rep 6 times. (30 sts)

Rnd 17: *Sc 3, dec 1*, rep 6 times. (24 sts)

Using pattern below, cut 4 medium mushroom spots of white felt and sew to mushroom cap.

Rnd 18: *Sc 2, dec 1*, rep 6 times. (18 sts)

Stuff.

Rnd 19: *Sc 1, dec 1*, rep 6 times. (12 sts)

Rnd 20: Dec 6 times, sl st 1. (6 sts)

Fasten off and weave in end.

Stem

Rnd 1: Using E hook and white yarn, ch 2, 5 sc in second ch from hook.

Rnd 2: Sc 2 in each sc around. (10 sts)

Rnd 3: *Sc 1, 2 sc in next sc*, rep 5 times. (15 sts)

Rnd 4: *Sc 2, 2 sc in next sc*, rep 5 times. (20 sts)

Rnd 5: *Sc 3, 2 sc in next sc*, rep 5 times. (25 sts)

Rnd 6: *Sc 4, 2 sc in next sc*, rep 5 times. (30 sts)

Rnd 7: Through back loops only, *sc 4, dec 1*, rep 5 times. (25 sts)

Rnds 8–12: Sc 25.

Fasten off, leaving long tail for sewing.

Position and attach eyes. Embroider mouth.

Stuff and sew stem to cap.

Large Mushroom

Cap

Rnd 1: Using F hook and red yarn, ch 2, 6 sc in second ch from hook.

Rnd 2: Sc 2 in each sc around. (12 sts)

Rnd 3: *Sc 1, 2 sc in next sc*, rep 6 times. (18 sts)

Rnd 4: *Sc 2, 2 sc in next sc*, rep 6 times. (24 sts)

Rnd 5: *Sc 3, 2 sc in next sc*, rep 6 times. (30 sts)

Rnd 6: *Sc 4, 2 sc in next sc*, rep 6 times. (36 sts)

Rnd 7: *Sc 5, 2 sc in next sc*, rep 6 times. (42 sts)

Rnd 8: *Sc 6, 2 sc in next sc*, rep 6 times. (48 sts)

Rnds 9–16: Sc 48.

Rnd 17: *Sc 6, dec 1*, rep 6 times. (42 sts)

Rnd 18: *Sc 5, dec 1*, rep 6 times. (36 sts)

Rnd 19: *Sc 4, dec 1*, rep 6 times. (30 sts)

Rnd 20: *Sc 3, dec 1*, rep 6 times. (24 sts)

Using pattern below, cut 4 large mushroom spots of white felt and sew to mushroom cap.

Rnd 21: *Sc 2, dec 1*, rep 6 times. (18 sts)

Stuff.

Rnd 22: *Sc 1, dec 1*, rep 6 times. (12 sts)

Rnd 23: Dec 6 times, sl st 1. (6 sts)

Fasten off and weave in end.

Stem

Rnd 1: Using E hook and white yarn, ch 2, 5 sc in second ch from hook.

Rnd 2: Sc 2 in each sc around. (10 sts)

Rnd 3: *Sc 1, 2 sc in next sc*, rep 5 times. (15 sts)

Rnd 4: *Sc 2, 2 sc in next sc*, rep 5 times. (20 sts)

Rnd 5: *Sc 3, 2 sc in next sc*, rep 5 times. (25 sts)

Rnd 6: *Sc 4, 2 sc in next sc*, rep 5 times. (30 sts)

Rnd 7: *Sc 5, 2 sc in next sc*, rep 5 times. (35 sts)

Rnd 8: Through back loops only, *sc 5, dec 1*, rep 5 times. (30 sts)

Rnds 9–13: Sc 30.

Fasten off, leaving long tail for sewing.

Position and attach eyes. Embroider mouth.

Stuff and sew stem to cap.

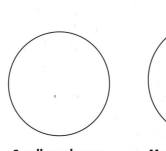

Small mushroom spot

Medium mushroom spot

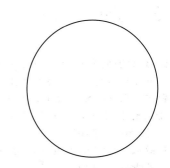

Large mushroom spot

Tea Set and Cookies

I've loved tea parties since I was a little girl, when I would go with my mom to her friend Graciela's house. There we'd have a little tea party with cookies and pastries (the best part of the tea) each time we visited, and they would let me have a cup of tea! Doesn't every girl love a tea party, even if it's made out of yarn?

Finished Sizes

Teapot: Approx 5" tall with lid
Sugar bowl: Approx 3" tall with lid
Cup: Approx 3" in diameter x 2" tall
Saucer: Approx 3½" in diameter
Spoon: Approx 3" long
Cookie plate: Approx 4¼" in diameter
Cookie: Approx 1¾" in diameter

Materials

Worsted-weight yarn in blue, yellow, tan, and a tiny bit of brown
Size F-5 (3.75 mm) crochet hook
Tapestry needle
A tiny bit of fiberfill or stuffing of your choice (for the teapot's handle and cookies)

Teapot

Pot

Rnd 1: Using blue yarn, ch 2, 6 sc in second ch from hook.
Rnd 2: Sc 2 in each sc around. (12 sts)
Rnd 3: *Sc 1, 2 sc in next sc*, rep 6 times. (18 sts)

Rnd 4: *Sc 2, 2 sc in next sc*, rep 6 times. (24 sts)
Rnd 5: *Sc 3, 2 sc in next sc*, rep 6 times. (30 sts)
Rnd 6: *Sc 4, 2 sc in next sc*, rep 6 times. (36 sts)
Rnd 7: *Sc 5, 2 sc in next sc*, rep 6 times. (42 sts)
Rnd 8: *Sc 6, 2 sc in next sc*, rep 6 times. (48 sts)
Rnd 9: *Sc 7, 2 sc in next sc*, rep 6 times. (54 sts)
Rnd 10: *Sc 8, 2 sc in next sc*, rep 6 times. (60 sts)
Rnds 11–17: Sc 60.
Rnd 18: Using yellow yarn, sc 60.
Rnd 19: Using blue yarn, sc 60.
Rnd 20: Using yellow yarn, sc 60.
Rnds 21–23: Using blue yarn, sc 60.
Rnd 24: *Sc 8, dec 1*, rep 6 times. (54 sts)
Rnd 25: Sc 54.
Rnd 26: *Sc 7, dec 1*, rep 6 times. (48 sts)
Rnd 27: Sc 48.
Rnd 28: *Sc 6, dec 1*, rep 6 times. (42 sts)
Rnd 29: Sc 42.

Rnd 30: BPsc 42.
Rnds 31 and 32: Sc 42.
Fasten off and weave in ends.

Lid

Rnd 1: Using yellow yarn, ch 2, 6 sc in second ch from hook.
Rnd 2: Sc 2 in each sc around. (12 sts)
Rnd 3: *Sc 1, 2 sc in next sc*, rep 6 times. (18 sts)
Rnd 4: *Sc 2, 2 sc in next sc*, rep 6 times. (24 sts)
Rnd 5: *Sc 3, 2 sc in next sc*, rep 6 times. (30 sts)

Rnd 6: *Sc 4, 2 sc in next sc*, rep
6 times. (36 sts)
Rnd 7: *Sc 5, 2 sc in next sc*, rep
6 times. (42 sts)
Rnds 8–12: Sc 42.
Fasten off and weave in ends.

Knob on Lid

Rnd 1: Using blue yarn, ch 2, 5 sc in
second ch from hook.
Rnd 2: Sc 2 in each sc around. (10 sts)
Rnd 3: *Sc 1, 2 sc in next sc*, rep
5 times. (15 sts)
Rnd 4: Sc 15.
Fasten off, leaving long tail for sewing.
Sew knob to top of lid.

Spout

Rnd 1: Using blue yarn and leaving
a long tail for sewing, ch 2, 6 sc in
second ch from hook.
Rnd 2: Sc 2 in each sc around. (12 sts)
Rnd 3: *Sc 1, 2 sc in next sc*, rep
6 times. (18 sts)
Rnds 4–6: Sc 18.
Rnd 7: *Sc 1, dec 1*, rep 6 times. (12 sts)
Rnds 8–11: Sc 12.
Fasten off and weave in ends. Sew
closed end of spout to teapot.

Handle

Rnd 1: Using blue yarn, ch 2, 5 sc in
second ch from hook.
Rnd 2: Sc 2 in each sc around. (10 sts)
Rnds 3–16: Sc 10, stuffing as you go.
Fasten off, leaving long tail for sewing.
Sew handle to pot.

Sugar Bowl

Bowl

Rnd 1: Using blue yarn, ch 2, 6 sc in
second ch from hook.
Rnd 2: Sc 2 in each sc around. (12 sts)
Rnd 3: *Sc 1, 2 sc in next sc*, rep
6 times. (18 sts)
Rnd 4: *Sc 2, 2 sc in next sc*, rep
6 times. (24 sts)
Rnd 5: *Sc 3, 2 sc in next sc*, rep
6 times. (30 sts)
Rnd 6: *Sc 4, 2 sc in next sc*, rep
6 times. (36 sts)
Rnd 7: *Sc 5, 2 sc in next sc*, rep
6 times. (42 sts)
Rnd 8: *Sc 6, 2 sc in next sc*, rep
6 times. (48 sts)
Rnds 9–13: Sc 48.
Rnd 14: Using yellow yarn, sc 48.
Rnds 15 and 16: Using blue yarn, sc 48.
Rnd 17: BPsc 48.
Rnds 18 and 19: Sc 48.
Fasten off and weave in ends.

Lid

Rnd 1: Using yellow yarn, ch 2, 6 sc in
second ch from hook.
Rnd 2: Sc 2 in each sc around. (12 sts)
Rnd 3: *Sc 1, 2 sc in next sc*, rep
6 times. (18 sts)
Rnd 4: *Sc 2, 2 sc in next sc*, rep
6 times. (24 sts)
Rnd 5: *Sc 3, 2 sc in next sc*, rep
6 times. (30 sts)
Rnd 6: *Sc 4, 2 sc in next sc*, rep
6 times. (36 sts)
Rnd 7: *Sc 5, 2 sc in next sc*, rep
6 times. (42 sts)
Rnd 8: *Sc 6, 2 sc in next sc*, rep
6 times. (48 sts)
Rnds 9–13: Sc 48.
Fasten off and weave in ends.

Knob on Lid

Using blue yarn, work as for knob on
teapot lid, left.

Cup and Saucer

Cup

Rnd 1: Using blue yarn, ch 2, 6 sc in second ch from hook.

Rnd 2: Sc 2 in each sc around. (12 sts)

Rnd 3: *Sc 1, 2 sc in next sc*, rep 6 times. (18 sts)

Rnd 4: *Sc 2, 2 sc in next sc*, rep 6 times. (24 sts)

Rnd 5: *Sc 3, 2 sc in next sc*, rep 6 times. (30 sts)

Rnd 6: *Sc 4, 2 sc in next sc*, rep 6 times. (36 sts)

Rnd 7: *Sc 5, 2 sc in next sc*, rep 6 times. (42 sts)

Rnd 8: *Sc 6, 2 sc in next sc*, rep 6 times. (48 sts)

Rnds 9–13: Sc 48.

Rnd 14: Using yellow yarn, sc 48.

Rnd 15: Using blue yarn, sc 48.

Rnd 16: Using yellow yarn, sc 48.

Rnds 17–19: Using blue yarn, sc 48.

Fasten off and weave in ends.

Handle

Rnd 1: Using blue yarn, ch 2, 5 sc in second ch from hook.

Rnds 2–12: Sc 5.

Fasten off, leaving long tail for sewing. Sew handle to cup.

Saucer

Rnd 1: Using yellow yarn, ch 2, 6 sc in second ch from hook.

Rnd 2: Sc 2 in each sc around. (12 sts).

Rnd 3: *Sc 1, 2 sc in next sc*, rep 6 times. (18 sts)

Rnd 4: *Sc 2, 2 sc in next sc*, rep 6 times. (24 sts)

Rnd 5: *Sc 3, 2 sc in next sc*, rep 6 times. (30 sts)

Rnd 6: *Sc 4, 2 sc in next sc*, rep 6 times. (36 sts)

Rnd 7: *Sc 5, 2 sc in next sc*, rep 6 times. (42 sts)

Rnd 8: *Sc 6, 2 sc in next sc*, rep 6 times. (48 sts)

Rnd 9: *Sc 7, 2 sc in next sc*, rep 6 times. (54 sts)

Rnds 10 and 11: Sc 54.

Fasten off and weave in end.

Spoon

Bowl of Spoon

Rnd 1: Using yellow yarn, ch 2, 5 sc in second ch from hook.

Rnd 2: Sc 2 in each sc around. (10 sts)

Rnd 3: *Sc 1, 2 sc in next sc*, rep 5 times. (15 sts)

Rnd 4: Sc 15.

Fasten off and weave in ends.

Handle

Rnd 1: Using yellow yarn, ch 2, 5 sc in second ch from hook.

Rnds 2–11: Sc 5.

Fasten off, leaving long tail for sewing. Sew handle to bowl of spoon.

Cookie Plate

Rnd 1: Using yellow yarn, ch 2, 6 sc in second ch from hook.

Rnd 2: Sc 2 in each sc around. (12 sts)

Rnd 3: *Sc 1, 2 sc in next sc*, rep 6 times. (18 sts)

Rnd 4: *Sc 2, 2 sc in next sc*, rep 6 times. (24 sts)

Rnd 5: *Sc 3, 2 sc in next sc*, rep 6 times. (30 sts)

Rnd 6: *Sc 4, 2 sc in next sc*, rep 6 times. (36 sts)

Rnd 7: *Sc 5, 2 sc in next sc*, rep 6 times. (42 sts)

Rnd 8: *Sc 6, 2 sc in next sc*, rep 6 times. (48 sts)

Rnd 9: *Sc 7, 2 sc in next sc*, rep 6 times. (54 sts)

Rnd 10: *Sc 8, 2 sc in next sc*, rep 6 times. (60 sts)

Rnd 11: *Sc 9, 2 sc in next sc*, rep 6 times. (66 sts)

Rnd 12: Using blue yarn, *sc 10, 2 sc in next sc*, rep 6 times. (72 sts)

Rnd 13: Using yellow yarn, sc 72.

Rnd 14: Using blue yarn, sc 72.

Fasten off and weave in ends.

Cookie

Make lots!

Rnd 1: Using tan yarn, ch 2, 5 sc in second ch from hook.

Rnd 2: Sc 2 in each sc around. (10 sts)

Rnd 3: *Sc 1, 2 sc in next sc*, rep 5 times. (15 sts)

Rnd 4: *Sc 2, 2 sc in next sc*, rep 6 times. (20 sts)

Rnd 5: *Sc 3, 2 sc in next sc*, rep 6 times. (25 sts)

Rnd 6: Sc 25.

Fasten off, leaving long tail for sewing. Embroider chocolate chips with brown yarn.

Rep rnds 1–6 for other side of cookie. Put 2 sides of cookie WS tog, stuff slightly and sew tog.

Hot-Dog Set

In Uruguay we call hot dogs *panchos*. They were my favorite food when I was growing up, but I would eat them with mashed potatoes instead of a bun! Our girls love to play with their pancho set, and they have lots of fun pretending to sell and buy them and asking each other if they want ketchup or mayonnaise (they don't like mustard).

Finished Sizes

Bun: Approx 6" long
Hot dog: Approx 7" long
Mustard bottle: Approx 3" tall
Ketchup bottle: Approx 4¾" tall

Materials

Worsted-weight yarn in white, tan, burgundy, red, and yellow
Size G-6 (4 mm) crochet hook
Plastic eyes with safety backings: 6 mm for hotdog, 9 mm for condiment bottles
Small pieces of yellow and red craft felt
Sewing thread and sharp needle
Black embroidery floss and embroidery needle
Tapestry needle
Fiberfill or stuffing of your choice

Bun

The bread is crocheted in the round—well, more like in the "oval."

Bottom

Make 2. These will look like 2 little canoes.
Using tan yarn, loosely ch 21.
Rnd 1: Sc 20 starting at second bump at back of ch (see "Working in Chain Loops," page 171), and then sc 20 on opposite side of ch (both loops of ch). (40 sts)
Rnd 2: *Sc 4 in next sc, sc 19*, rep once. (46 sts)
Rnd 3: *Sc 2 in each of next 3 sc, sc 20*, rep once. (52 sts)
Rnd 4: *Sc 2 in each of next 4 sc, sc 22*, rep once. (60 sts)
Rnd 5: *Sc 2 in each of next 5 sc, sc 25*, rep once. (72 sts)
Rnds 6–10: Sc 70.
Fasten off and set aside.

Top

Make 2. These will look like surfboards. Using white yarn, work rnds 1–5 as for bottom.

Rnd 6: Sc 70.

Fasten off, leaving long tail for sewing. With WS tog, align sts of 1 bottom with sts of 1 top and sew tog, stuffing as you go (don't worry if the top looks smaller than the bottom, because they're the same amount of sts; once you start sewing, they'll look perfect). Repeat for other top and bottom pieces. Use tan yarn to sew 2 halves tog along sides so they look like a real hot-dog bun.

Hot Dog (*el Pancho!*)

Rnd 1: Using burgundy yarn, ch 2, 5 sc in second ch from hook.

Rnd 2: Sc 2 in each sc around. (10 sts)

Rnd 3: *Sc 1, sc 2 in next sc*, rep 5 times. (15 sts)

Rnds 4–12: Sc 15.

Position and attach 6 mm eyes; embroider mouth. Use pattern on page 118 to cut 2 cheeks from yellow felt and sew them to face.

Rnds 13–40: Sc 15, stuffing as you go.

Rnd 41: *Sc 1, dec 1*, rep 5 times. (10 sts)

Rnd 42: Dec 5 times. (5 sts)

Fasten off, leaving long tail to close 5-st hole.

Mustard Bottle

Rnd 1: Using yellow yarn, ch 2, 6 sc in second ch from hook.

Rnd 2: Sc 2 in each st around. (12 sts)

Rnd 3: *Sc 1, 2 sc in next st*, rep 6 times. (18 sts)

Rnd 4: *Sc 2, 2 sc in next st*, rep 6 times. (24 sts)

Rnd 5: *Sc 3, 2 sc in next st*, rep 6 times. (30 sts)

Rnd 6: *Sc 4, 2 sc in next st*, rep 6 times. (36 sts)

Rnd 7: Through back loops only, *sc 4, dec 1*, rep 6 times. (30 sts)

Rnds 8–16: Sc 30.

Rnd 17: Sc 30 through back loops only.

Rnd 18: *Sc 3, dec 1*, rep 6 times. (24 sts)

Rnd 19: *Sc 2, dec 1*, rep 6 times. (18 sts)

Position and attach 9 mm eyes; embroider mouth. Use pattern, right, to cut 2 cheeks from red felt and sew them to face.

Rnd 20: *Sc 1, dec 1*, rep 6 times. (12 sts)

Rnd 21: Sc 12.

Stuff almost to top.

Rnd 22: Dec 6 times. (6 sts)

Rnd 23: Sc 6.

Sl st 1 and fasten off, leaving long tail to close up 6-st hole.

Ketchup Bottle

Rnd 1: Using red yarn, ch 2, 6 sc in second ch from hook.

Rnd 2: Sc 2 in each st around. (12 sts)

Rnd 3: *Sc 1, 2 sc in next st*, rep 6 times. (18 sts)

Rnd 4: *Sc 2, 2 sc in next st*, rep 6 times. (24 sts)

Rnd 5: *Sc 3, 2 sc in next st*, rep 6 times. (30 sts)

Rnd 6: Through back loops only, *sc 3, dec 1*, rep 6 times. (24 sts)

Rnds 7–24: Sc 24.

Position and attach 9 mm eyes; embroider mouth.

Rnd 25: Sc 24 through back loops only.

Rnd 26: *Sc 2, dec 1*, rep 6 times. (18 sts)

Rnd 27: *Sc 1, dec 1*, rep 6 times. (12 sts)

Rnd 28: Sc 12.

Stuff almost to top.

Rnd 29: Dec 6 times. (6 sts)

Rnd 30: Sc 6.

Sl st 1 and fasten off, leaving long tail to close up 6-st hole.

Hot dog cheek

Mustard bottle cheek

Mom and Baby Polar Bears

I enjoy spending time doing things together with my girls. Oli loves sewing buttons on little pieces of fabric, embroidering, and crocheting. (You should see my glowing face right now.) Martina loves to help me bake, and also likes drawing and playing with dolls. I bet you that mom and baby polar bears just love to fish together!

Finished Sizes

Mom polar bear: Approx 5½" tall
Baby polar bear: Approx 3½" tall

Materials

Worsted-weight yarn in white, orange, green, gray, and brown
Size G-6 (4 mm) and F-5 (3.75 mm) crochet hooks (use G hook unless otherwise instructed)
Plastic eyes with safety backings: 9 mm for baby and 12 mm for mom
Small piece of blue craft felt
Black embroidery floss and embroidery needle
Tapestry needle
Fiberfill or stuffing of your choice
1 pipe cleaner

Mom Polar Bear

Use white yarn throughout for Mom.

Muzzle

Rnd 1: Ch 2, 5 sc in second ch from hook.

Rnd 2: Sc 2 in each sc around. (10 sts)
Rnd 3: *Sc 1, 2 sc in next sc*, rep 5 times. (15 sts)
Rnd 4: Sc 15.
Sl st 1 and fasten off, leaving long tail for sewing. Embroider nose and mouth and set aside.

Head

Rnd 1: Ch 2, 5 sc in second ch from hook.
Rnd 2: Sc 2 in each sc around. (10 sts)
Rnd 3: *Sc 1, 2 sc in next sc*, rep 5 times. (15 sts)
Rnd 4: *Sc 2, 2 sc in next sc*, rep 5 times. (20 sts)
Rnd 5: *Sc 3, 2 sc in next sc*, rep 5 times. (25 sts)
Rnd 6: *Sc 4, 2 sc in next sc*, rep 5 times. (30 sts)
Rnd 7: *Sc 5, 2 sc in next sc*, rep 5 times. (35 sts)
Rnd 8: *Sc 6, 2 sc in next sc*, rep 5 times. (40 sts)
Rnds 9–17: Sc 40.
Rnd 18: *Sc 6, dec 1*, rep 5 times. (35 sts)
Rnd 19: *Sc 5, dec 1*, rep 5 times. (30 sts)
Rnd 20: *Sc 4, dec 1*, rep 5 times. (25 sts)
Using the pattern on page 123, cut 2 circles from blue felt. Cut small slit in middle of each circle, insert 12 mm eyes, and secure to head. Stuff muzzle slightly and sew to face.

Rnd 21: *Sc 3, dec 1*, rep 5 times. (20 sts)

Rnd 22: *Sc 2, dec 1*, rep 5 times. (15 sts) Stuff head.

Rnd 23: *Sc 1, dec 1*, rep 5 times. (10 sts)

Rnd 24: Dec 5 times. (5 sts) Fasten off, and set aside.

Ears

Make 2.

Rnd 1: Ch 2, 6 sc in second ch from hook.

Rnds 2 and 3: Sc 6.

Sl st 1 and fasten off, leaving long tail for sewing. Sew open end closed and sew to head.

Body

Rnd 1: Ch 2, 5 sc in second ch from hook.

Rnd 2: Sc 2 in each sc around. (10 sts)

Rnd 3: *Sc 1, 2 sc in next sc*, rep 5 times. (15 sts)

Rnd 4: *Sc 2, 2 sc in next sc*, rep 5 times. (20 sts)

Rnd 5: *Sc 3, 2 sc in next sc*, rep 5 times. (25 sts)

Rnds 6–17: Sc 25.

Sl st 1 and fasten off, leaving long tail for sewing. Stuff and sew to head.

Arms and Legs

Make 4.

Rnd 1: Ch 2, 5 sc in second ch from hook.

Rnd 2: Sc 2 in each sc around. (10 sts)

Rnds 3–10: Sc 10.

Fasten off, leaving long tail for sewing. Stuff, sew open end closed, and sew to body.

Mom's Hat

Rnd 1: Using orange yarn, ch 2, 6 sc in second ch from hook.

Rnd 2: Sc 2 in each sc around. (12 sts)

Rnd 3: *Sc 1, 2 sc in next sc*, rep 6 times. (18 sts)

Rnd 4: *Sc 2, 2 sc in next sc*, rep 6 times. (24 sts)

Rnd 5: *Sc 3, 2 sc in next sc*, rep 6 times. (30 sts)

Rnd 6: *Sc 4, 2 sc in next sc*, rep 6 times. (36 sts)

Rnd 7: *Sc 5, 2 sc in next sc*, rep 6 times. (42 sts)

Rnds 8–16: Sc 42.

Rnd 17: Sc 8, hdc 1, dc 2, tr 2, dc 2, hdc 1, sc 13, hdc 1, dc 2, tr 2, dc 2, hdc 1, sc 5.

Rnd 18: Change to green yarn, sc 42. Sl st 1 and fasten off.

Pom-pom: Referrring to "Pom-Pom" on page 123, make a pom-pom approx 1½" in diameter using green yarn and sew it on top of hat.

Ties: Join green yarn to a sc right under one of the trebles in rnd 17. Loosely ch 33. Starting at se cond ch from hook, sl st 32 and join to hat with sl st. Fasten off. Rep on other side.

Baby Polar Bear

Use white yarn throughout for Baby.

Muzzle

Rnd 1: Ch 2, 6 sc in second ch from hook.

Rnd 2: Sc 2 in each sc around. (12 sts)

Rnd 3: Sc 12.

Sl st 1 and fasten off, leaving long tail for sewing. Embroider nose and mouth and set aside.

Head

Rnd 1: Ch 2, 5 sc in second ch from hook.

Rnd 2: Sc 2 in each sc around. (10 sts)

Rnd 3: *Sc 1, 2 sc in next sc*, rep 5 times. (15 sts)

Rnd 4: *Sc 2, 2 sc in next sc*, rep 5 times. (20 sts)

Rnd 5: *Sc 3, 2 sc in next sc*, rep 5 times. (25 sts)

Rnd 6: *Sc 4, 2 sc in next sc*, rep 5 times. (30 sts)

Rnds 7–13: Sc 30.

Rnd 14: *Sc 4, dec 1*, rep 5 times. (25 sts)

Position and attach 9 mm eyes; stuff muzzle a little and sew to face.

Rnd 15: *Sc 3, dec 1*, rep 5 times. (20 sts)

Body

Rnd 1: Ch 2, 5 sc in second ch from hook.

Rnd 2: Sc 2 in each sc around. (10 sts)

Rnd 3: *Sc 1, 2 sc in next sc*, rep 5 times. (15 sts)

Rnd 4: *Sc 2, 2 sc in next sc*, rep 5 times. (20 sts)

Rnds 5–10: Sc 20.

Sl st 1 and fasten off, leaving long tail for sewing. Stuff and sew to head.

Arms and Legs (Make 4.)

Rnd 1: Ch 2, 6 sc in second ch from hook.

Rnds 2–7: Sc 6.

Sl st 1 and fasten off, leaving long tail for sewing. Sew open end closed and sew to body.

Fishing Pole

Use brown yarn throughout.

Long Branch

Rnd 1: Ch 2, 5 sc in second ch from hook.

Rnds 2–23: Sc 5.

Sl st 1 and fasten off, leaving long tail for sewing. Slip pipe cleaner inside pole so it's stronger; cut off extra pipe cleaner. Sew open end closed.

Little Branch

Rnd 1: Ch 2, 5 sc in second ch from hook.

Rnds 2 and 3: Sc 5.

Sl st 1 and fasten off, leaving long tail for sewing. Sew to pole.

Rnd 16: *Sc 2, dec 1*, rep 5 times. (15 sts)

Stuff head.

Rnd 17: *Sc 1, dec 1*, rep 5 times. (10 sts)

Rnd 18: Dec 5 times. (5 sts)

Fasten off, and set aside.

Ears

Make 2.

Rnd 1: Ch 2, 5 sc in second ch from hook.

Rnds 2 and 3: Sc 5.

Sl st 1 and fasten off, leaving long tail for sewing. Sew open end closed and sew to head.

Fish

Make 2. Use F hook and gray yarn for body and tail.

Body

Rnd 1: Ch 2, 5 sc in second ch from hook.
Rnd 2: Sc 2 in each sc around. (10 sts)
Rnds 3–5: Sc 10.
Rnd 6: Dec 5 times. (5 sts)
Sl st 1 and fasten off, leaving long tail for sewing. Sew open end closed.

Tail

Make 4.
Ch 6, dc 1 in third ch from hook, hdc 1, sc 1, sl st 1, rep once.
Sl st 1 and fasten off. Sew 2 tails to each body.

Finishing

Cut piece of orange yarn (as long as you want the line), tie one end to end of pole, and sew other end to fish's mouth. Sew other fish to baby's arms.

Mom polar bear eye

Pom-Pom

1. Cut two circles from cardboard, 1½" in diameter. Cut hole in center of each circle, about ¾" in diameter. Thread long piece of yarn through tapestry needle. Hold two circles together, insert needle into hole, wrap it around, and then back through hole. Repeat, working evenly around circle, rethreading needle when necessary until circle is filled completely. When you think you have it full enough, add some more. The fuller, the better!

2. Use sharp scissors to cut yarn around edge between two pieces of cardboard.

3. Cut 12"-long piece of yarn. Run this yarn between the cardboard circles and tie very tightly. Slide circles off pom-pom and fluff it out, trimming any stray ends.

Garden Friends:
Snake, Mouse, and Bird

Some months ago we moved to a house after living in apartments for the longest time. Now we get to play outside more and have garden friends. Thankfully we haven't seen any snakes or mice, but lots of cute birds visit our backyard every morning!

Finished Sizes

Snake: Approx 12½" long
Mouse: Approx 3" long
Bird on stump: Approx 4" tall

Materials

Worsted-weight yarn in red, brown, green, light pink, dark pink, and gray
Size G-6 (4 mm), F-5 (3.75 mm), and E-4 (3.5 mm) crochet hooks
Plastic eyes with safety backings: 6 mm for bird and mouse, 9 mm for snake
Small pieces of pink and tan craft felt
Sewing thread and sharp needle
Black and pink embroidery floss and embroidery needle
Tapestry needle
Fiberfill or stuffing of your choice

Snake

Head

Rnd 1: Using G hook and green yarn, ch 2, 6 sc in second ch from hook.
Rnd 2: Sc 2 in each sc around. (12 sts)

Rnd 3: *Sc 1, 2 sc in next sc*, rep 6 times. (18 sts)
Rnd 4: *Sc 2, 2 sc in next sc*, rep 6 times. (24 sts)
Rnds 5–10: Sc 24.
Rnd 11: *Sc 2, dec 1*, rep 6 times. (18 sts)
Position and attach 9 mm eyes; embroider mouth with black embroidery floss. Using pattern on page 128, cut snake tongue from pink felt and sew below mouth.
Rnd 12: *Sc 1, dec 1*, rep 6 times. (12 sts)
Stuff head.
Rnd 13: Dec 6 times. (6 sts)
Sl st 1 and fasten off, leaving long tail for sewing, and set aside.

Body

Rnd 1: Using green yarn, ch 2, 4 sc in second ch from hook.
Rnd 2: Sc 4.
Rnd 3: Sc 2 in each sc around. (8 sc)
Rnd 4: Sc 8.

Rnd 5: Using dark-pink yarn, sc 8.
Begin alternating 4 rows of green and 1 row of pink (ending with 4 rows of green).
Rnds 6–59: Sc 8, stuffing very lightly as you go.
Sl st 1 and fasten off, leaving long tail for sewing. Sew body to head.

Mouse

Start crocheting the mouse at the nose.

Body

Rnd 1: Using F hook and gray yarn, ch 2, 5 sc in second ch from hook.

Rnd 2: Sc 2 in each sc around. (10 sts)

Rnd 3: Sc 10.

Rnd 4: *Sc 1, 2 sc in next sc*, rep 5 times. (15 sts)

Rnd 5: Sc 15.

Rnd 6: *Sc 2, 2 sc in next sc*, rep 5 times. (20 sts)

Rnd 7: Sc 20.

Rnd 8: *Sc 3, 2 sc in next sc*, rep 5 times. (25 sts)

Position and attach 6 mm eyes. Embroider nose with pink embroidery floss and mouth with black embroidery floss.

Rnds 9–15: Sc 25.

Rnd 16: *Sc 3, dec 1*, rep 5 times. (20 sts)

Rnd 17: *Sc 2, dec 1*, rep 5 times. (15 sts)

Rnd 18: Sc 15.

Rnd 19: *Sc 1, dec 1*, rep 5 times. (10 sts)

Stuff.

Rnd 20: Dec 5 times. (5 sts)

Fasten off.

Ears

Make 2.

Using F hook and gray yarn, ch 2, 8 sc in second ch from hook.

Fasten off, leaving long tail for sewing. Sew ears to body.

Front Legs

Make 2.

Rnd 1: Using E hook and light-pink yarn, ch 2, 4 sc in second ch from hook.

Rnds 2–4: Sc 4.

Sl st 1 and fasten off, leaving long tail for sewing. Sew open end closed and sew legs to body.

Back Legs

Make 2.

Rnd 1: Using E hook and light-pink yarn, ch 2, 6 sc in second ch from hook.

Rnds 2–4: Sc 6.

Sl st 1 and fasten off, leaving long tail for sewing. Sew legs to body.

Tail

Using F hook and light-pink yarn, loosely ch 25. Starting in second ch from hook, sl st 24.

Fasten off, leaving long tail for sewing. Sew tail to body.

Bird

Use F hook and red yarn throughout for bird.

Head

Rnd 1: Ch 2, 6 sc in second ch from hook.

Rnd 2: Sc 2 in each sc. (12 sts)

Rnd 3: *Sc 1, 2 sc in next sc*, rep 6 times. (18 sts)

Rnd 4: *Sc 2, 2 sc in next sc*, rep 6 times. (24 sts)

Rnds 5–10: Sc 24.

Wings

Make 2.

Rnd 1: Ch 2, 5 sc in second ch from hook.

Rnd 2: Sc 2 in each sc around. (10 sts)

Rnds 3–8: Sc 10.

Rnd 9: Dec 5 times. (5 sts)

Sl st 1 and fasten off, leaving long tail for sewing. Sew open end closed and sew wings to body.

Tail

Make 2.

Rnd 1: Ch 2, 6 sc in second ch from hook.

Rnds 2–8: Sc 6.

Sl st 1 and fasten off, leaving long tail for sewing. Sew tail to body.

Rnd 11: *Sc 2, dec 1*, rep 6 times. (18 sts)

Position and attach 6 mm eyes. Using pattern on page 128, cut bird beak from tan felt, fold in half, and sew to face.

Rnd 12: *Sc 1, dec 1*, rep 6 times. (12 sts)

Stuff head firmly.

Rnd 13: Dec 6 times. (6 sts)

Fasten off and set aside.

Body

Rnd 1: Ch 2, 6 sc in second ch from hook.

Rnd 2: Sc 2 in each sc around. (12 sts)

Rnd 3: *Sc 1, 2 sc in next sc*, rep 6 times. (18 sts)

Rnds 4–7: Sc 18.

Sl st 1 and fasten off, leaving long tail for sewing. Stuff firmly and sew body to head.

Stump

Rnd 1: Using F hook and brown yarn, ch 2, 6 sc in second ch from hook.

Rnd 2: Sc 2 in each sc around. (12 sts)

Rnd 3: *Sc 1, 2 sc in next sc*, rep 6 times. (18 sts)

Rnd 4: *Sc 2, 2 sc in next sc*, rep 6 times. (24 sts)

Rnd 5: *Sc 3, 2 sc in next sc*, rep 6 times. (30 sts)

Rnd 6: *Sc 4, 2 sc in next sc*, rep 6 times. (36 sts)

Rnd 7: Sc 36 through back loops only.

Rnds 8–14: Sc 36.

Rnd 15: *Sc 5, 2 sc in next sc*, rep 6 times. (42 sts)

Rnd 16: Through back loops only, *sc 5, dec 1*, rep 6 times. (36 sts)

Rnd 17: *Sc 4, dec 1*, rep 6 times. (30 sts)

Rnd 18: *Sc 3, dec 1*, rep 6 times. (24 sts)

Rnd 19: *Sc 2, dec 1*, rep 6 times. (18 sts)

Stuff.

Rnd 20: *Sc 1, dec 1*, rep 6 times. (12 sts)

Rnd 21: *Sk 1 sc, sc 1*, rep 6 times. (6 sts)

Fasten off.

Little Branch

Rnd 1: Using F hook and brown yarn, ch 2, 4 sc in second ch from hook.

Rnd 2: Sc 2 in each sc. (8 sts)

Rnds 3 and 4: Sc 8.

Sl st 1 and fasten off, leaving long tail for sewing. Stuff and sew branch to stump.

Leaf

Using F hook and green yarn, loosely ch 5. Starting at second ch from hook, sl st 1, dc 2, sl st 1.

Fasten off, leaving long tail for sewing. Sew leaf to branch.

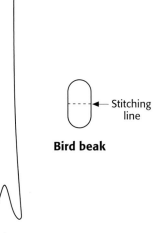

← Stitching line

Bird beak

Snake tongue

Little Bunny and Her Carrot Home

Wouldn't you love to be surrounded by your favorite food? I imagine myself in a big room full of *dulce de leche* . . . and the ideal home for a little bunny would definitely be a carrot! This would make a really cute Easter present; fill the carrot with jelly beans and sit the bunny on top for a super-sweet surprise.

Finished Sizes

Bunny: Approx 3" tall
Carrot: Approx 7" long when closed

Materials

Worsted-weight yarn in orange, green, and white
Size F-5 (3.75 mm) crochet hook
6 mm plastic eyes with safety backings
Pink embroidery floss and embroidery needle
Tapestry needle
Fiberfill or stuffing of your choice

Carrot

Top

Rnd 1: Using orange yarn, ch 2, 6 sc in second ch from hook.
Rnd 2: Sc 2 in every sc around. (12 sts)
Rnd 3: *Sc 1, 2 sc in next sc*, rep 6 times. (18 sts)
Rnd 4: *Sc 2, 2 sc in next sc*, rep 6 times. (24 sts)
Rnd 5: *Sc 3, 2 sc in next sc*, rep 6 times. (30 sts)
Rnd 6: *Sc 4, 2 sc in next sc*, rep 6 times. (36 sts)

Rnd 7: *Sc 5, 2 sc in next sc*, rep 6 times. (42 sts)
Rnd 8: *Sc 6, 2 sc in next sc*, rep 6 times. (48 sts)
Rnds 9–15: Sc 48.
Rnd 16: *Sc 6, dec 1*, rep 6 times. (42 sts)
Rnd 17: BPsc 42.
Rnd 18: Sc 42.
Sl st 1 and fasten off.

Bottom

Rnd 1: Using orange yarn, ch 2, 6 sc in second ch from hook.
Rnd 2: Sc 2 in every sc around. (12 sts)
Rnd 3: *Sc 1, 2 sc in next sc*, rep 6 times. (18 sts)
Rnds 4–6: Sc 18.
Rnd 7: *Sc 2, 2 sc in next sc*, rep 6 times. (24 sts)
Rnds 8–10: Sc 24.

Rnd 11: *Sc 3, 2 sc in next sc*, rep 6 times. (30 sts)

Rnds 12–14: Sc 30.

Rnd 15: *Sc 4, 2 sc in next sc*, rep 6 times. (36 sts)

Rnds 16–20: Sc 36.

Rnd 21: *Sc 5, 2 sc in next sc*, rep 6 times. (42 sts)

Rnds 22–26: Sc 42.

Rnd 27: *Sc 6, 2 sc in next sc*, rep 6 times. (48 sts)

Rnds 28–32: Sc 48.

Sl st 1 and fasten off.

Leaves

Make 6.

Using green yarn, loosely ch 14. Starting at third ch from hook, 11 hdc, 5 hdc in next ch. You are now on other side of ch (just below what you just crocheted), 12 hdc.

Fasten off, leaving long tail for sewing. Sew leaves to top of carrot as shown on page 130.

Little Bunny

Use white yarn throughout.

Head

Rnd 1: Ch 2, 6 sc in second ch from hook.

Rnd 2: Sc 2 in each sc around. (12 sts)

Rnd 3: *Sc 1, 2 sc in next sc*, rep 6 times. (18 sts)

Rnd 4: *Sc 2, 2 sc in next sc*, rep 6 times. (24 sts)

Rnds 5–11: Sc 24.

Rnd 12: *Sc 2, dec 1*, rep 6 times. (18 sts)

Position and attach eyes; embroider mouth and nose.

Rnd 13: *Sc 1, dec 1*, rep 6 times. (12 sts)

Stuff.

Rnd 14: *Sk 1 sc, sc 1*, rep 6 times. (6 sts)

Fasten off.

Ears

Make 2.

Rnd 1: Ch 2, 6 sc in second ch from hook.

Rnds 2–4: Sc 6.

Sl st 1 and fasten off, leaving long tail for sewing. Sew to top of head.

Body

Rnd 1: Ch 2, 6 sc in second ch from hook.

Rnd 2: Sc 2 in each sc around. (12 sts)

Rnd 3: *Sc 1, 2 sc in next sc*, rep 6 times. (18 sts)

Rnds 4–8: Sc 18.

Sl st 1 and fasten off, leaving long tail for sewing. Stuff and sew to head.

Legs and Arms

Make 4.

Rnd 1: Ch 2, 5 sc in second ch from hook.

Rnds 2–4: Sc 5.

Sl st 1 and fasten off, leaving long tail for sewing. Sew open end closed and sew to body.

Sea Friends:
Jellyfish, Cuttlefish, Dolphin, and Little Narwhal

I used to like animated movies, but after watching them over and over with my girls, I'm tired of their little voices and happy speech. To my surprise, however, there came, *Ponyo*, one of the sweetest movies for kids (and adults!) on the planet. We've seen it lots of times, and the sea theme just kept coming to my mind while planning this batch of ocean-inspired toys.

Finished Sizes

Jellyfish: Approx 10" long including tentacles
Cuttlefish: Approx 5" long
Dolphin: Approx 7½" long
Narwhal: Approx 7" long

Materials

Worsted-weight yarn in pink, blue, gray, and white
Size G-6 (4 mm) and F-5 (3.75 mm) crochet hooks (F hook is used only for narwhal's tusk)
Plastic eyes with safety backings: 9 mm for narwol; 12 mm for cuttlefish, dolphin, and jellyfish
Black embroidery floss and embroidery needle
Tapestry needle
Fiberfill or stuffing of your choice

Jellyfish

Use G hook and pink yarn throughout.

Body

Rnd 1: Ch 2, 6 sc in second ch from hook.
Rnd 2: Sc 2 in each sc around. (12 sts)
Rnd 3: *Sc 1, 2 sc in next sc*, rep 6 times. (18 sts)
Rnd 4: *Sc 2, 2 sc in next sc*, rep 6 times. (24 sts)
Rnds 5 and 6: Sc 24.
Rnd 7: *Sc 3, 2 sc in next sc*, rep 6 times. (30 sts)
Rnd 8: Sc 30.
Rnd 9: *Sc 4, 2 sc in next sc*, rep 6 times. (36 sts)
Rnd 10: *Sc 5, 2 sc in next sc*, rep 6 times. (42 sts)
Rnds 11–18: Sc 42.

Rnd 19: Sc 42 through back loops only. (You'll use front loops later when crocheting the wavy bottom edge.) Position and attach 12 mm eyes; embroider mouth.

Rnd 20: *Sc 5, dec 1*, rep 6 times. (36 sts)

Rnd 21: *Sc 4, dec 1*, rep 6 times. (30 sts)

Rnd 22: *Sc 3, dec 1*, rep 6 times. (24 sts)

Rnd 23: *Sc 2, dec 1*, rep 6 times. (18 sts)

Rnd 24: *Sc 1, dec 1*, rep 6 times. (12 sts)

Stuff firmly.

Rnd 25: Dec 6 times. (6 sts)

Fasten off, leaving long tail to close 6-st hole.

Holding body upside down and starting at back, join yarn to a front loop you left in rnd 19, then *hdc 4 in next st, sk 1 st, sl st 1*, rep from * to * all around body. Fasten off.

Tentacles

Inner tentacles: Make 3. Loosely ch 42. Starting at third ch from hook, hdc 40. Fasten off, leaving long tail for sewing. When you have all 3, sew them tog, and then sew them to middle of bottom of body.

Outer tentacles: Make 6. Loosely ch 37. Starting at second ch from hook, *sc 2, sk 1 st, sc 2, sc 3 in next st*, rep from * to *. Fasten off, leaving long tail for sewing. Sew outer tentacles to bottom, spacing them evenly around inner tentacles.

Cuttlefish

Use G hook throughout.

Eye Roundies

Make 2.

Rnd 1: Using white yarn, ch 2, 6 sc in second ch from hook.

Rnd 2: Sc 2 in each sc around. (12 sts)

Sl st 1 and fasten off, leaving long tail for sewing. Insert 12 mm eye through middle hole and set aside.

Body

Rnd 1: Using blue yarn, ch 2, 6 sc in second ch from hook.

Rnd 2: Sc 2 in each sc around. (12 sts)

Rnd 3: *Sc 1, 2 sc in next sc*, rep 6 times. (18 sts)

Rnd 4: Sc 18.

Rnd 5: *Sc 2, 2 sc in next sc*, rep 6 times. (24 sts)

Rnd 6: Sc 24.

Rnd 7: *Sc 3, 2 sc in next sc*, rep 6 times. (30 sts)

Rnds 8 and 9: Sc 30.

Rnd 10: *Sc 4, 2 sc in next sc*, rep 6 times. (36 sts)

Rnds 11–22: Sc 36.

Sl st 1 and fasten off.

Position and attach eyes (with eye roundies), sew eye roundies in place, and embroider mouth.

Base

Rnd 1: Using blue yarn, ch 2, 6 sc in second ch from hook.

Rnd 2: Sc 2 in each sc around. (12 sts)

Rnd 3: *Sc 1, 2 sc in next sc*, rep 6 times. (18 sts)

Rnd 4: *Sc 2, 2 sc in next sc*, rep 6 times. (24 sts)

Rnd 5: *Sc 3, 2 sc in next sc*, rep 6 times. (30 sts)

Rnd 6: *Sc 4, 2 sc in next sc*, rep 6 times. (36 sts)

Sl st 1 and fasten off, leaving long tail for sewing. Stuff body and sew base to top to close up the body.

Legs

Make 8.

Rnd 1: Using blue yarn, ch 2, 4 sc in second ch from hook.

Rnd 2: Sc 2 in each sc around. (8 sts)

Rnds 3–6: Sc 8.

Sl st 1 and fasten off, leaving long tail for sewing. Stuff and sew legs to base as shown on page 134.

Dolphin

Use G hook throughout.

Eye Roundies

Make 2.

Rnd 1: Using blue yarn, ch 2, 5 sc in second ch from hook.

Rnd 2: Sc 2 in each sc around. (10 sts)

Rnd 3: *Sc 1, 2 sc in next sc*, rep 5 times. (15 sts)

Rnd 4: *Sc 2, 2 sc in next sc*, rep 5 times. (20 sts)

Sl st 1 and fasten off, leaving long tail for sewing. Insert 12 mm eye through middle hole and set aside.

Snout

Rnd 1: Using gray yarn, ch 2, 5 sc in second ch from hook.

Rnd 2: Sc 2 in each sc around. (10 sts)

Rnd 3: Sc 10.

Rnd 4: *Sc 1, 2 sc in next sc*, rep 5 times. (15 sts)

Rnds 5–7: Sc 15.

Sl st 1 and fasten off, leaving long tail for sewing. Embroider line around edge of snout (for dolphin's mouth). Stuff lightly and set aside.

Body

Rnd 1: Using gray yarn, ch 2, 5 sc in second ch from hook.

Rnd 2: Sc 2 in each sc around. (10 sts)

Rnd 3: *Sc 1, 2 sc in next sc*, rep 5 times. (15 sts)

Rnd 4: *Sc 2, 2 sc in next sc*, rep 5 times. (20 sts)

Rnd 5: *Sc 3, 2 sc in next sc*, rep 5 times. (25 sts)

Rnd 6: *Sc 4, 2 sc in next sc*, rep 5 times. (30 sts)

Rnd 7: *Sc 5, 2 sc in next sc*, rep 5 times. (35 sts)

Rnds 8–11: Sc 35.

Rnd 12: *Sc 5, dec 1*, rep 5 times. (30 sts)

Rnds 13–16: Sc 30.

Position and attach eyes (with eye roundies); sew roundies in place. Flatten snout and sew to face.

Rnds 17 and 18: Sc 30.

Rnd 19: *Sc 4, dec 1*, rep 5 times. (25 sts)

Rnds 20 and 21: Sc 25.

Rnd 22: *Sc 3, dec 1*, rep 5 times. (20 sts)

Rnds 23–26: Sc 20.

Rnd 27: *Sc 2, dec 1*, rep 5 times. (15 sts)

Rnd 28: Sc 15.

Stuff firmly.

Rnd 29: *Sc 1, dec 1*, rep 5 times. (10 sts)

Rnd 30: Dec 5 times.

Sl st 1 and fasten off.

Pectoral Flippers

Make 2.

Rnd 1: Using gray yarn, ch 2, 6 sc in second ch from hook.

Rnd 2: Sc 6.

Rnd 3: Sc 2 in each sc around. (12 sts)

Rnds 4–6: Sc 12.

Sl st 1 and fasten off, leaving long tail for sewing. Sew open end closed and sew fins to sides of body.

Dorsal Fin

Rnd 1: Using gray yarn, ch 2, 5 sc in second ch from hook.

Rnd 2: Sc 5.

Rnd 3: Sc 2 in each sc around. (10 sts)

Rnds 4 and 5: Sc 10.

Sl st 1 and fasten off, leaving long tail for sewing. Sew fin to top of body.

Tail Fins

Make 2.

Rnd 1: Using gray yarn, ch 2, 5 sc in second ch from hook.

Rnd 2: Sc 5.

Rnd 3: Sc 2 in each sc around. (10 sts)

Rnds 4–7: Sc 10.

Rnd 8: Dec 5 times. (5 sts)

Sl st 1 and fasten off, leaving long tail for sewing. Sew fins to body.

Little Narwhal

Use G hook, except for tusk.

Eye Roundies

Make 2.

Rnd 1: Using white yarn, ch 2, 6 sc in second ch from hook.

Rnd 2: Sc 2 in each sc around. (12 sts)

Sl st 1 and fasten off, leaving long tail for sewing. Insert 9 mm eye through center and set aside.

Body

Rnd 1: Using blue yarn, ch 2, 5 sc in second ch from hook.

Rnd 2: Sc 2 in each sc around. (10 sts)

Rnd 3: *Sc 1, 2 sc in next sc*, rep 5 times. (15 sts)

Rnd 4: *Sc 2, 2 sc in next sc*, rep 5 times. (20 sts)

Rnd 5: *Sc 3, 2 sc in next sc*, rep 5 times. (25 sts)

Rnds 6–12: Sc 25.

Position and attach eyes (with eye roundies); sew eye roundies in place. Embroider mouth.

Rnd 13: *Sc 3, dec 1*, rep 5 times. (20 sts)

Rnds 14–16: Sc 20.

Rnd 17: *Sc 2, dec 1*, rep 5 times. (15 sts)

Rnds 18–21: Sc 15.

Stuff almost to top.

Rnd 22: *Sc 1, dec 1*, rep 5 times. (10 sts)

Rnd 23: Sc 10.

Rnd 24: *Sk 1 sc, sc 1*, rep 5 times. (5 sts)

Sl st 1 and fasten off.

Flippers

Make 2.

Rnd 1: Using blue yarn, ch 2, 5 sc in second ch from hook.

Rnd 2: Sc 5.

Rnd 3: Sc 2 in each sc around. (10 sts)

Rnds 4 and 5: Sc 10.

Sl st 1 and fasten off, leaving long tail for sewing. Sew open end closed and sew flippers to sides of body.

Tail Fins

Make 2.

Rnd 1: Using blue yarn, ch 2, 5 sc in second ch from hook.

Rnd 2: Sc 5.

Rnd 3: Sc 2 in each sc around. (10 sts)

Rnds 4–6: Sc 10.

Rnd 7: Dec 5 times. (5 sts)

Sl st 1 and fasten off, leaving long tail for sewing. Sew open end closed and sew fins to body.

Tusk

Rnd 1: Using F hook and white yarn, ch 2, 4 sc in second ch from hook.

Rnd 2: Sc 4.

Rnd 3: Sc 2 in each sc around. (8 sts)

Rnds 4–9: Sc 8, stuffing as you go.

Sl st 1 and fasten off, leaving long tail for sewing. Sew tusk to face.

Santiago, My Little Boston Terrier

Santiago is my first dog ever. I'd been wanting a dog for as long as I can remember. I never thought you could love a dog so much! I'm amazed at how smart and loving he is.

Finished Sizes

Boston terrier: Approx 5" tall
Bed: Approx 4½" diameter

Materials

Worsted-weight yarn in black, white, and red
Size G-6 (4 mm) crochet hook
12 mm plastic eyes with safety backings
Black embroidery floss and embroidery needle
Tapestry needle
Fiberfill or stuffing of your choice

Santiago

Muzzle

Rnd 1: Using white yarn, ch 2, 6 sc in second ch from hook.
Rnd 2: Sc 2 in each sc around. (12 sts)
Rnd 3: *Sc 1, 2 sc in next sc*, rep 6 times. (18 sts)
Rnds 4 and 5: Sc 18.
Sl st 1 and fasten off, leaving long tail for sewing. Embroider nose and mouth and set aside.

Stripe above Muzzle

Using white yarn and working back and forth, loosely ch 4.
Row 1: Sc 3, starting in second ch from hook.
Rows 2 and 3: Ch 1, sc 3, turn.
Row 4: Ch 1, 2 sc in next sc, sc 1, 2 sc in next sc, turn. (5 sts)
Row 5: Ch 1, sc 5.
Fasten off, leaving long tail for sewing, and set aside.

Head

Rnd 1: Using black yarn, ch 2, 7 sc in second ch from hook.
Rnd 2: Sc 2 in each sc around. (14 sts)
Rnd 3: *Sc 1, 2 sc in next sc*, rep 7 times. (21 sts)
Rnd 4: *Sc 2, 2 sc in next sc*, rep 7 times. (28 sts)
Rnd 5: *Sc 3, 2 sc in next sc*, rep 7 times. (35 sts)
Rnds 6–14: Sc 35.
Rnd 15: *Sc 3, dec 1*, rep 7 times. (28 sts)
Rnds 16 and 17: Sc 28.
Stuff muzzle a little and sew to face. Sew white stripe to head (making sure wider end is at top). Position and attach eyes.

Rnd 18: *Sc 2, dec 1*, rep 7 times. (21 sts)
Rnd 19: *Sc 1, dec 1*, rep 7 times. (14 sts)
Stuff firmly.
Rnd 20: Dec 7 times. (7 sts)
Fasten off.

Ears

Make 2.
Rnd 1: Using black yarn, ch 2, 4 sc in second ch from hook.
Rnd 2: Sc 2 in each sc around. (8 sts)
Rnd 3: Sc 8.
Rnd 4: *Sc 1, 2 sc in next sc*, rep 4 times. (12 sts)
Rnds 5–8: Sc 12.
Sl st 1 and fasten off, leaving long tail for sewing. Sew ears to head.

Body

Rnd 1: Using black yarn, ch 2, 7 sc in second ch from hook.
Rnd 2: Sc 2 in each sc around. (14 sts)
Rnd 3: *Sc 1, 2 sc in next sc*, rep 7 times. (21 sts)
Rnds 4–8: Sc 21.
Rnds 9–11: Using white yarn, sc 21.
Sl st 1 and fasten off, leaving long tail for sewing. Stuff body and sew to head.

Legs

Make 2 using black for back legs and 2 using white for front legs.

Rnd 1: Ch 2, 5 sc in second ch from hook.

Rnd 2: Sc 2 in each sc around. (10 sts)

Rnds 3–5: Sc 10.

Change to black if you started with white for front legs; cont with black for back legs.

Rnds 6–10: Sc 10.

Sl st 1 and fasten off, leaving long tail for sewing. Stuff lightly, sew open end closed, and sew legs to body.

Bed and Pillow

Use red yarn for both.

Bed

Rnd 1: Ch 2, 5 sc in second ch from hook.

Rnd 2: Sc 2 in each sc around. (10 sts)

Rnd 3: *Sc 1, 2 sc in next sc*, rep 5 times. (15 sts)

Rnd 4: *Sc 2, 2 sc in next sc*, rep 5 times. (20 sts)

Rnd 5: *Sc 3, 2 sc in next sc*, rep 5 times. (25 sts)

Rnd 6: *Sc 4, 2 sc in next sc*, rep 5 times. (30 sts)

Rnd 7: *Sc 5, 2 sc in next sc*, rep 5 times. (35 sts)

Rnd 8: *Sc 6, 2 sc in next sc*, rep 5 times. (40 sts)

Rnd 9: *Sc 7, 2 sc in next sc*, rep 5 times. (45 sts)

Rnd 10: *Sc 8, 2 sc in next sc*, rep 5 times. (50 sts)

Rnd 11: *Sc 9, 2 sc in next sc*, rep 5 times. (55 sts)

Rnd 12: *Sc 10, 2 sc in next sc*, rep 5 times. (60 sts)

Rnd 13: Sc 60.

Rnd 14: Sc 60 through back loops only.

Rnds 15–21: Sc 60.

Sl st 1 and fasten off.

Pillow

Work rnds 1–11 as for bed.

Rnd 12: Sc 55.

Sl st 1 and fasten off.

Make another circle for other side of pillow. With WS tog, align sts of 2 circles, sew approx three-quarters of the way around, stuff lightly, and finish sewing. Let your puppy take a nap!

I love to see baby ducks and their moms walking in a line, and I think they would look extra cute with little hats on, especially bear and apple hats!

Finished Sizes

Mom duck: Approx 5" tall
Baby duck: Approx 3½" tall

Materials

Worsted-weight yarn in white, yellow, orange, red, brown, and green
Size G-6 (4 mm) crochet hook
Plastic eyes with safety backings: 9 mm for baby and 12 mm for mom
Tapestry needle
Fiberfill or stuffing of your choice

Mom Duck

Beak

Rnd 1: Using orange yarn, ch 2, 7 sc in second ch from hook.
Rnd 2: Sc 2 in each sc around. (14 sts)
Rnds 3–5: Sc 14.
Sl st 1 and fasten off, leaving long tail for sewing, and set aside.

Head

Rnd 1: Using white yarn, ch 2, 6 sc in second ch from hook.
Rnd 2: Sc 2 in each sc around. (12 sts)
Rnd 3: *Sc 1, 2 sc in next sc*, rep 6 times. (18 sts)
Rnd 4: *Sc 2, 2 sc in next sc*, rep 6 times. (24 sts)
Rnd 5: *Sc 3, 2 sc in next sc*, rep 6 times. (30 sts)
Rnd 6: *Sc 4, 2 sc in next sc*, rep 6 times. (36 sts)
Rnd 7: *Sc 5, 2 sc in next sc*, rep 6 times. (42 sts)
Rnds 8–16: Sc 42.
Rnd 17: *Sc 5, dec 1*, rep 6 times. (36 sts)
Rnd 18: *Sc 4, dec 1*, rep 6 times. (30 sts)
Rnd 19: *Sc 3, dec 1*, rep 6 times. (24 sts)
Rnd 20: Sc 24.
Sew beak in place; position and attach 12 mm eyes.
Rnd 21: *Sc 2, dec 1*, rep 6 times. (18 sts)
Rnd 22: *Sc 1, dec 1*, rep 6 times. (12 sts)
Stuff head firmly.
Rnd 23: *Sk 1 sc, sc 1*, rep 6 times. (6 sts)
Fasten off.

Body

Rnd 1: Using white yarn, ch 2, 5 sc in second ch from hook.
Rnd 2: Sc 2 in each sc around. (10 sts)
Rnd 3: *Sc 1, 2 sc in next sc*, rep 5 times. (15 sts)
Rnd 4: *Sc 2, 2 sc in next sc*, rep 5 times. (20 sts)
Rnd 5: *Sc 3, 2 sc in next sc*, rep 5 times. (25 sts)
Rnds 6–13: Sc 25.
Sl st 1 and fasten off, leaving long tail for sewing. Stuff body and sew to head.

Wings

Make 2.
Rnd 1: Using white yarn, ch 2, 5 sc in second ch from hook.
Rnd 2: Sc 2 in each sc around. (10 sts)
Rnd 3: *Sc 1, 2 sc in next sc*, rep 5 times. (15 sts)

Rnds 4–7: Sc 15.

Sl st 1 and fasten off, leaving long tail for sewing. Sew open end closed and sew wings to body.

Feet

Make 2.

Rnd 1: Using orange yarn, ch 2, 7 sc in second ch from hook.

Rnd 2: Sc 2 in each sc around. (14 sts)

Rnds 3–7: Sc 14.

Sl st 1 and fasten off, leaving long tail for sewing. Sew open end closed and sew feet to body.

Mom's Apple Hat

Rnd 1: Using red yarn, ch 2, 6 sc in second ch from hook.

Rnd 2: Sc 2 in each sc around. (12 sts)

Rnd 3: *Sc 1, 2 sc in next sc*, rep 6 times. (18 sts)

Rnd 4: *Sc 2, 2 sc in next sc*, rep 6 times. (24 sts)

Rnd 5: *Sc 3, 2 sc in next sc*, rep 6 times. (30 sts)

Rnd 6: *Sc 4, 2 sc in next sc*, rep 6 times. (36 sts)

Rnd 7: *Sc 5, 2 sc in next sc*, rep 6 times. (42 sts)

Rnd 8: *Sc 6, 2 sc in next sc*, rep 6 times. (48 sts)

Rnds 9–15: Sc 48.

Sl st 1 and fasten off.

Stem: Using brown yarn, loosely ch 5. Starting at second ch from hook, sl st 4. Fasten off, leaving long tail for sewing. Sew stem to hat.

Leaf: Using green yarn, loosely ch 10. Starting at second ch from hook, sl st 1, hdc 1, dc 1, tr 3, dc 1, hdc 1, sl st 1. Fasten off, leaving long tail for sewing. Sew leaf next to stem.

Baby Duck

Beak

Rnd 1: Using orange yarn, ch 2, 5 sc in second ch from hook.

Rnd 2: Sc 2 in each sc around. (10 sts)

Rnd 3: Sc 10.

Sl st 1 and fasten off, leaving long tail for sewing, and set aside.

Head

Rnd 1: Using yellow yarn, ch 2, 6 sc in second ch from hook.

Rnd 2: Sc 2 in each sc around. (12 sts)

Rnd 3: *Sc 1, 2 sc in next sc*, rep 6 times. (18 sts)

Rnd 4: *Sc 2, 2 sc in next sc*, rep 6 times. (24 sts)

Rnd 5: *Sc 3, 2 sc in next sc*, rep 6 times. (30 sts)

Rnds 6–12: Sc 30.

Rnd 13: *Sc 3, dec 1*, rep 6 times. (24 sts)

Rnd 14: *Sc 2, dec 1*, rep 6 times. (18 sts)

Rnd 15: Sc 18.

Sew beak in place; position and attach 9 mm eyes.

Rnd 16: *Sc 1, dec 1*, rep 6 times. (12 sts)

Stuff head firmly.

Rnd 17: *Sk 1 sc, sc 1*, rep 6 times. (6 sts)

Fasten off.

Body

Rnd 1: Using yellow yarn, ch 2, 6 sc in second ch from hook.

Rnd 2: Sc 2 in each sc around. (12 sts)

Rnd 3: *Sc 1, 2 sc in next sc*, rep 6 times. (18 sts)

Rnds 4–9: Sc 18.

Fasten off, leaving long tail for sewing. Stuff and sew body to head.

Wings

Make 2.

Rnd 1: Using yellow yarn, ch 2, 4 sc in second ch from hook.

Rnd 2: Sc 2 in each sc around. (8 sts)

Rnds 3–5: Sc 8.

Sl st 1 and fasten off, leaving long tail for sewing. Sew open end closed and sew wings to body.

Feet

Make 2.

Rnd 1: Using orange yarn, ch 2, 5 sc in second ch from hook.

Rnd 2: Sc 2 in each sc around. (10 sts)

Rnds 3–5: Sc 10.

Sl st 1 and fasten off, leaving long tail for sewing. Sew open end closed and sew feet to body.

Baby's Bear Hat

Rnd 1: Using brown yarn, ch 2, 6 sc in second ch from hook.

Rnd 2: Sc 2 in each sc around. (12 sts)

Rnd 3: *Sc 1, 2 sc in next sc*, rep 6 times. (18 sts)

Rnd 4: *Sc 2, 2 sc in next sc*, rep 6 times. (24 sts)

Rnd 5: *Sc 3, 2 sc in next sc*, rep 6 times. (30 sts)

Rnd 6: *Sc 4, 2 sc in next sc*, rep 6 times. (36 sts)

Rnds 7–10: Sc 36.

Sl st 1 and fasten off.

Ears: Ch 2, 8 sc in second ch from hook. Fasten off, leaving long tail for sewing. Make 2 and sew to hat.

When Oli was little she really liked pigs. I think it's because she also really liked everything and anything that was pink. She slept with a little stuffed piggy for years. It just seemed fitting to make this little pig and give him a mom and a little vest.

Finished Sizes

Mom pig: Approx 7" tall
Little pig: Approx 4½" tall

Materials

Worsted-weight yarn in pink, red, white, and tan
Size G-6 (4 mm) and F-5 (3.75 mm) crochet hooks
Plastic eyes with safety backings: 9 mm for baby, 12 mm for mom
Small piece of black craft felt
Black embroidery floss and embroidery needle
Tapestry needle
Fiberfill or stuffing of your choice

Mom Pig

Use G hook throughout.

Muzzle

Rnd 1: Using pink yarn, ch 2, 6 sc in second ch from hook.
Rnd 2: Sc 2 in each sc around. (12 sts)
Rnd 3: *Sc 1, 2 sc in next sc*, rep 6 times. (18 sts)
Rnd 4: Sc 18.

Sl st 1 and fasten off, leaving long tail for sewing. Using the pattern on page 148, cut 2 nostrils from black felt and sew to muzzle. Set muzzle aside.

Eye Roundies

Make 2.
Rnd 1: Using white yarn, ch 2, 5 sc in second ch from hook.
Rnd 2: Sc 2 in each sc around. (10 sts)

Rnd 3: *Sc 1, 2 sc in next sc*, rep 5 times. (15 sts)
Sl st 1 and fasten off, leaving long tail for sewing. Insert 12 mm eye through middle hole and set aside.

Head

Rnd 1: Using pink yarn, ch 2, 6 sc in second ch from hook.
Rnd 2: Sc 2 in each sc around. (12 sts)

Rnd 3: *Sc 1, 2 sc in next sc*, rep 6 times. (18 sts)

Rnd 4: *Sc 2, 2 sc in next sc*, rep 6 times. (24 sts)

Rnd 5: *Sc 3, 2 sc in next sc*, rep 6 times. (30 sts)

Rnd 6: *Sc 4, 2 sc in next sc*, rep 6 times. (36 sts)

Rnd 7: *Sc 5, 2 sc in next sc*, rep 6 times. (42 sts)

Rnds 8–17: Sc 42.

Rnd 18: *Sc 5, dec 1*, rep 6 times. (36 sts)

Rnd 19: *Sc 4, dec 1*, rep 6 times. (30 sts)

Rnd 20: *Sc 3, dec 1*, rep 6 times. (24 sts)

Rnd 21: Sc 24.

Stuff muzzle slightly and sew to face. Position and attach eyes (with eye roundies); sew eye roundies in place.

Rnd 22: *Sc 2, dec 1*, rep 6 times. (18 sts)

Rnd 23: *Sc 1, dec 1*, rep 6 times. (12 sts)

Stuff head firmly.

Rnd 24: Dec 6 times. (6 sts)

Fasten off.

Ears

Make 2.

Rnd 1: Using pink yarn, ch 2, 6 sc in second ch from hook.

Rnd 2: Sc 6.

Rnd 3: Sc 2 in each sc around. (12 sts)

Rnds 4 and 5: Sc 12.

Sl st 1 and fasten off, leaving long tail for sewing. Sew open end closed and sew to head.

Body

Rnd 1: Using pink yarn, ch 2, 5 sc in second ch from hook.

Rnd 2: Sc 2 in each sc around. (10 sts)

Rnd 3: *Sc 1, 2 sc in next sc*, rep 5 times. (15 sts)

Rnd 4: *Sc 2, 2 sc in next sc*, rep 5 times. (20 sts)

Rnd 5: *Sc 3, 2 sc in next sc*, rep 5 times. (25 sts)

Rnds 6–9: Sc 25.

Change to red and alternate 1 row red and 1 row white to end.

Rnds 10–16: Sc 25.

Sl st 1 and fasten off, leaving long tail for sewing. Stuff body and sew to head.

Arms and Legs

Make 4.

Rnd 1: Using pink yarn, ch 2, 5 sc in second ch from hook.

Rnd 2: Sc 2 in each sc around. (10 sts)

Rnds 3–10: Sc 10.

Sl st 1 and fasten off, leaving long tail for sewing. Stuff, sew open end of arms closed, and then sew arms and legs to body.

Little Pig

Use F hook throughout.

Muzzle

Rnd 1: Using tan yarn, ch 2, 6 sc in second ch from hook.

Rnd 2: Sc 2 in each sc around. (12 sts)

Rnd 3: *Sc 1, 2 sc in next sc*, rep 6 times. (18 sts)

Rnd 4: Sc 18.

Sl st 1 and fasten off, leaving long tail for sewing. Using the pattern on page 148, cut 2 nostrils from black felt and sew to muzzle. Set muzzle aside.

Eye Roundies

Make 2.

Rnd 1: Using white yarn, ch 2, 6 sc in second ch from hook.

Rnd 2: Sc 2 in each sc around. (12 sts)

Sl st 1 and fasten off, leaving long tail for sewing. Insert 9 mm eye through middle hole and set aside.

Head

Rnd 1: Using tan yarn, ch 2, 6 sc in second ch from hook.
Rnd 2: Sc 2 in each sc around. (12 sts)
Rnd 3: *Sc 1, 2 sc in next sc*, rep 6 times. (18 sts)
Rnd 4: *Sc 2, 2 sc in next sc*, rep 6 times. (24 sts)
Rnd 5: *Sc 3, 2 sc in next sc*, rep 6 times. (30 sts)
Rnds 6–12: Sc 30.
Rnd 13: *Sc 3, dec 1*, rep 6 times. (24 sts)
Rnd 14: *Sc 2, dec 1*, rep 6 times. (18 sts)
Rnds 15 and 16: Sc 18.
Stuff muzzle slightly and sew to face. Position and attach eyes (with eye roundies) and sew roundies in place.
Rnd 17: *Sc 1, dec 1*, rep 6 times. (12 sts)
Stuff firmly.
Rnd 18: Dec 6 times. (6 sts)
Fasten off.

Ears

Make 2.
Rnd 1: Using tan yarn, ch 2, 6 sc in second ch from hook.
Rnd 2: Sc 6.
Rnd 3: Sc 2 in each sc around. (12 sts)
Rnd 4: Sc 12.
Sl st 1 and fasten off, leaving long tail for sewing. Sew open end closed and sew ears to head.

Body

Rnd 1: Using tan yarn, ch 2, 6 sc in second ch from hook.
Rnd 2: Sc 2 in each sc around. (12 sts)
Rnd 3: *Sc 1, 2 sc in next sc*, rep 6 times. (18 sts)
Rnds 4–10: Sc 18.
Sl st 1 and fasten off, leaving long tail for sewing. Stuff body and sew to head.

Arms and Legs

Make 4.
Rnd 1: Using tan yarn, ch 2, 6 sc in second ch from hook.
Rnd 2–5: Sc 6.
Sl st 1 and fasten off, leaving long tail for sewing. Sew open end closed of arms only; then sew arms and legs to body.

Vest

Using red yarn, loosely ch 23.
Row 1: Starting at second ch from hook, sc 22. (22 sts)
Row 2: Ch 1, sc 3, ch 5, sk 5 sts, sc 6, ch 5, sk 5 sts, sc 3, turn.
Row 3: Ch 1, sc 3, sc 5 in 5-sp ch, sc 6, sc 5 in 5-sp ch, sc 3, turn. (22 sts)
Row 4: Ch 1, sc 22, turn.
Fasten off.
Ties: Join yarn to top corner of vest, ch 16, fasten off. Rep on opposite side.
Put vest on baby pig and secure ties at neck.

Pig nostril

I think koalas have to be among the sweetest–looking animals. I sewed the little baby to the mom's back, but you could attach Velcro on the baby's hands and the mom's back so the baby can be removed to go out and play!

Finished Sizes

Mom koala: Approx 5" tall
Baby koala: Approx 3" tall

Materials

Worsted-weight yarn in gray, white, and pink
Size G-6 (4 mm) crochet hook
Plastic eyes with safety backings: 9 mm for baby, 12 mm for mom
Small piece of black craft felt
Black embroidery floss and embroidery needle
Tapestry needle
Fiberfill or stuffing of your choice

Mom Koala

Eye Roundies

Make 2.
Rnd 1: Using white yarn, ch 2, 6 sc in second ch from hook.
Rnd 2: Sc 2 in each sc around. (12 sts)
Sl st 1 and fasten off, leaving long tail for sewing. Insert 12 mm eye through middle hole and set aside.

Head

Rnd 1: Using gray yarn, ch 2, 5 sc in second ch from hook.
Rnd 2: Sc 2 in each sc around. (10 sts)
Rnd 3: *Sc 1, 2 sc in next sc*, rep 5 times. (15 sts)
Rnd 4: *Sc 2, 2 sc in next sc*, rep 5 times. (20 sts)
Rnd 5: *Sc 3, 2 sc in next sc*, rep 5 times. (25 sts)
Rnd 6: *Sc 4, 2 sc in next sc*, rep 5 times. (30 sts)
Rnd 7: *Sc 5, 2 sc in next sc*, rep 5 times. (35 sts)
Rnd 8: *Sc 6, 2 sc in next sc*, rep 5 times. (40 sts)
Rnds 9–17: Sc 40.
Rnd 18: *Sc 6, dec 1*, rep 5 times. (35 sts)
Rnd 19: *Sc 5, dec 1*, rep 5 times. (30 sts)
Rnd 20: Sc 30.
Position and attach eyes (with eye roundies) and sew roundies in place. Using the pattern on page 151 to cut nose from black felt and sew in place; embroider mouth.
Rnd 21: *Sc 4, dec 1*, rep 5 times. (25 sts)
Rnd 22: *Sc 3, dec 1*, rep 5 times. (20 sts)
Rnd 23: *Sc 2, dec 1*, rep 5 times. (15 sts)
Stuff head.
Rnd 24: *Sc 1, dec 1*, rep 5 times. (10 sts)
Rnd 25: Dec 5 times. (5 sts)
Fasten off.

Ears

Make 2.
Rnd 1: Using gray yarn, ch 2, 5 sc in second ch from hook.
Rnd 2: Sc 2 in each sc around. (10 sts)
Rnd 3: *Sc 1, 2 sc in next sc*, rep 5 times. (15 sts)
Rnds 4 and 5: Sc 15.
Sl st 1 and fasten off, leaving long tail for sewing. Sew open end closed and sew ears to head.

Body

Rnd 1: Using gray yarn, ch 2, 5 sc in second ch from hook.
Rnd 2: Sc 2 in each sc around. (10 sts)
Rnd 3: *Sc 1, 2 sc in next sc*, rep 5 times. (15 sts)
Rnd 4: *Sc 2, 2 sc in next sc*, rep 5 times. (20 sts)
Rnd 5: *Sc 3, 2 sc in next sc*, rep 5 times. (25 sts)
Rnds 6–14: Sc 25.
Sl st 1 and fasten off, leaving long tail for sewing. Stuff body and sew to head.

Arms and Legs

Make 4.

Rnd 1: Using gray yarn, ch 2, 5 sc in second ch from hook.

Rnd 2: Sc 2 in each sc around. (10 sts)

Rnds 3–9: Sc 10.

Sl st 1 and fasten off, leaving long tail for sewing. Stuff, sew open end closed, and sew arms and legs to body.

Baby Koala

Eye Roundies

Make 2.

Rnd 1: Using white yarn, ch 2, 5 sc in second ch from hook.

Rnd 2: Sc 2 in each sc around. (10 sts)

Sl st 1 and fasten off, leaving long tail for sewing. Insert 9 mm eye through middle hole and set aside.

Head

Rnd 1: Using gray yarn, ch 2, 5 sc in second ch from hook.

Rnd 2: Sc 2 in each sc around. (10 sts)

Rnd 3: *Sc 1, 2 sc in next sc*, rep 5 times. (15 sts)

Rnd 4: *Sc 2, 2 sc in next sc*, rep 5 times. (20 sts)

Rnd 5: *Sc 3, 2 sc in next sc*, rep 5 times. (25 sts)

Rnds 6–11: Sc 25.

Rnd 12: *Sc 3, dec 1*, rep 5 times. (20 sts)

Position and attach eyes (with eye roundies) and sew roundies in place. Using the pattern, right, cut nose

from black felt and sew in place. Embroider mouth.

Rnd 13: *Sc 2, dec 1*, rep 5 times. (15 sts)

Rnd 14: *Sc 1, dec 1*, rep 5 times. (10 sts)

Stuff head.

Rnd 15: Dec 5 times. (5 sts)

Fasten off.

Ears

Make 2.

Rnd 1: Using gray yarn, ch 2, 5 sc in second ch from hook.

Rnd 2: Sc 2 in each sc around. (10 sts)

Rnds 3 and 4: Sc 10.

Sl st 1 and fasten off, leaving long tail for sewing. Sew ears to head.

Body

Rnd 1: Using pink yarn, ch 2, 5 sc in second ch from hook.

Rnd 2: Sc 2 in each sc around. (10 sts)

Rnd 3: *Sc 1, 2 sc in next sc*, rep 5 times. (15 sts)

Rnds 4–7: Sc 15.

Sl st 1 and fasten off, leaving long tail for sewing. Stuff body and sew to head.

Arms and Legs

Make 4.

Rnd 1: Using gray yarn, ch 2, 5 sc in second ch from hook.

Rnds 2–5: Sc 5.

Sl st 1 and fasten off, leaving long tail for sewing. Sew open end closed and sew arms and legs to body. Sew baby's arms to mommy's neck.

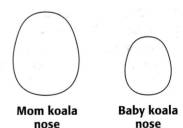

Mom koala nose   **Baby koala nose**

Little Kitten and Bed

Oli's allergic to cats, so this is the closest she can get to one without her eyes turning all puffy and red. When she was little, my friends would ask her if she had any allergies before giving her a snack, and she would say "Cats." My friends used to tease me, saying it sounded like we actually fed her cats!

Finished Sizes

Little kitten: Approx 4" long, not including tail
Bed: Approx 4½" diameter

Materials

Worsted-weight yarn in tan, white, and yellow (plus scrap for yarn ball)
Size F-5 (3.75 mm) and G-6 (4 mm) crochet hooks
9 mm plastic eyes with safety backings
Black embroidery floss and embroidery needle
Tapestry needle
Fiberfill or stuffing of your choice

Little Kitten

Use F hook throughout.

Muzzle

Rnd 1: Using white yarn, ch 2, 5 sc in second ch from hook.
Rnd 2: Sc 2 in each sc around. (10 sts)
Rnd 3: *Sc 1, 2 sc in next sc*, rep 5 times. (15 sts)
Rnd 4: Sc 15.

Sl st 1 and fasten off, leaving long tail for sewing. Embroider nose, mouth, and whiskers and set aside.

Head

Rnd 1: Using tan yarn, ch 2, 5 sc in second ch from hook.
Rnd 2: Sc 2 in each sc around. (10 sts)
Rnd 3: *Sc 1, 2 sc in next sc*, rep 5 times. (15 sts)
Rnd 4: *Sc 2, 2 sc in next sc*, rep 5 times. (20 sts)

Rnd 5: *Sc 3, 2 sc in next sc*, rep 5 times. (25 sts)
Rnd 6: *Sc 4, 2 sc in next sc*, rep 5 times. (30 sts)
Rnds 7–13: Sc 30.
Rnd 14: *Sc 4, dec 1*, rep 5 times. (25 sts)
Rnd 15: *Sc 3, dec 1*, rep 5 times. (20 sts)

Sew muzzle in place. Position and attach eyes.

Rnd 16: *Sc 2, dec 1, rep 5 times. (15 sts)

Rnd 17: *Sc 1, dec 1, rep 5 times. (10 sts)

Stuff firmly.

Rnd 18: Dec 5 times. (5 sts)

Fasten off.

Ears

Make 2.

Rnd 1: Using tan yarn, ch 2, 5 sc in second ch from hook.

Rnd 2: Sc 5.

Rnd 3: Sc 2 in each sc around. (10 sts)

Sl st 1 and fasten off, leaving long tail for sewing. Sew open end closed and sew ears to head.

Body

Rnd 1: Using tan yarn, ch 2, 5 sc in second ch from hook.

Rnd 2: Sc 2 in each sc around. (10 sts)

Rnd 3: *Sc 1, 2 sc in next sc*, rep 5 times. (15 sts)

Rnds 4–9: Sc 15.

Sl st 1 and fasten off, leaving long tail for sewing. Stuff and sew to head.

Legs

Make 4. Use tan yarn for one leg and white for the others.

Rnd 1: Ch 2, sc 5 in second ch from hook.

Rnds 2–5: Sc 5.

Sl st 1 and fasten off, leaving long tail for sewing. Sew open end closed and sew legs to body.

Tail

Rnd 1: Using tan yarn, ch 2, sc 5 in second ch from hook.

Rnds 2 and 3: Sc 5.

Rnds 4–11: Using white yarn, sc 5.

Sl st 1 and fasten off, leaving long tail for sewing. Sew tail to body.

Bed

Rnd 1: Using G hook and yellow yarn, ch 2, 6 sc in second ch from hook.

Rnd 2: Sc 2 in each sc around. (12 sts)

Rnd 3: *Sc 1, 2 sc in next sc*, rep 6 times. (18 sts)

Rnd 4: *Sc 2, 2 sc in next sc*, rep 6 times. (24 sts)

Rnd 5: *Sc 3, 2 sc in next sc*, rep 6 times. (30 sts)

Rnd 6: *Sc 4, 2 sc in next sc*, rep 6 times. (36 sts)

Rnd 7: *Sc 5, 2 sc in next sc*, rep 6 times. (42 sts)

Rnd 8: *Sc 6, 2 sc in next sc*, rep 6 times. (48 sts)

Rnd 9: *Sc 7, 2 sc in next sc*, rep 6 times. (54 sts)

Rnd 10: *Sc 8, 2 sc in next sc*, rep 6 times. (60 sts)

Rnds 11–20: Sc 60.

Sl st 1 and fasten off, leaving long tail for sewing. With RS facing you, fold edge over all around and sew edge to WS along row 12 of bed, stuffing lightly as you go.

Finishing

Make a little ball of yarn for your kitty to play with while she's tucked in her bed.

Princess Frog and Water Lily Throne

As much as Oli likes pigs, Martina loves frogs, which kind of surprised me at first because frogs don't seem very cute and cuddly to me. She also loves pretending to be a princess, with lots of jewelry and dresses, so a princess frog with a really cute— and pink!—throne seemed more than appropriate for her.

Finished Sizes

Princess frog: Approx 4" tall
Water lily throne: Approx 2½" tall

Materials

Worsted-weight yarn in green, yellow, and pink
Size G-6 (4 mm) crochet hook
9 mm plastic eyes with safety backings
Black embroidery floss and embroidery needle
Tapestry needle
Fiberfill or stuffing of your choice

Princess Frog

Use green yarn throughout.

Eyes

Make 2.
Rnd 1: Ch 2, 6 sc in second ch from hook.
Rnd 2: Sc 2 in each sc around. (12 sts)
Rnds 3–5: Sc 12.
Sl st 1 and fasten off, leaving long tail for sewing. Position and attach eyes, stuff, and set aside.

Head

Rnd 1: Ch 2, 6 sc in second ch from hook.
Rnd 2: Sc 2 in each sc around. (12 sts)
Rnd 3: *Sc 1, 2 sc in next sc*, rep 6 times. (18 sts)
Rnd 4: *Sc 2, 2 sc in next sc*, rep 6 times. (24 sts)
Rnd 5: *Sc 3, 2 sc in next sc*, rep 6 times. (30 sts)
Rnd 6: *Sc 4, 2 sc in next sc*, rep 6 times. (36 sts)
Rnds 7–12: Sc 36.
Sew eyes in place. Embroider mouth.
Rnd 13: *Sc 4, dec 1*, rep 6 times. (30 sts)
Rnd 14: *Sc 3, dec 1*, rep 6 times. (24 sts)
Rnd 15: *Sc 2, dec 1*, rep 6 times. (18 sts)
Rnd 16: *Sc 1, dec 1*, rep 6 times. (12 sts)
Stuff head.
Rnd 17: Dec 6 times. (6 sts)
Fasten off.

Body

Rnd 1: Ch 2, 6 sc in second ch from hook.
Rnd 2: Sc 2 in each sc around. (12 sts)
Rnd 3: *Sc 1, 2 sc in next sc*, rep 6 times. (18 sts)
Rnd 4: *Sc 2, 2 sc in next sc*, rep 6 times. (24 sts)
Rnds 5–10: Sc 24.
Sl st 1 and fasten off, leaving long tail for sewing. Stuff and sew to head.

Arms and Legs

Make 4.

Rnd 1: Ch 2, 6 sc in second ch from hook.

Rnds 2–6: Sc 6.

Sl st 1 and fasten off, leaving long tail for sewing. Sew open end closed and sew arms and legs to body.

Crown

Using yellow yarn, loosely ch 10, close with sl st to form a ring.

Rnd 1: Sc 10 inside ring.

Rnd 2: *Sl st 1, dc 1*, rep all around.

Sl st 1 and fasten off, leaving long tail for sewing. Sew crown to frog's head.

Water Lily Throne

Cushion

Rnd 1: Using yellow yarn, ch 2, 5 sc in second ch from hook.

Rnd 2: Sc 2 in each sc around. (10 sts)

Rnd 3: *Sc 1, 2 sc in next sc*, rep 5 times. (15 sts)

Rnd 4: *Sc 2, 2 sc in next sc*, rep 5 times. (20 sts)

Rnd 5: *Sc 3, 2 sc in next sc*, rep 5 times. (25 sts)

Rnd 6: *Sc 4, 2 sc in next sc*, rep 5 times. (30 sts)

Rnd 7: *Sc 5, 2 sc in next sc*, rep 5 times. (35 sts)

Rnd 8: Sc 35.

Rnd 9: Sc 35 through back loops only.

Rnd 10: Sc 35.

Rnd 11: Sc 35 through back loops only.

Rnd 12: Sc 35.

Rnd 13: *Sc 5, dec 1*, rep 5 times. (30 sts)

Rnd 14: *Sc 4, dec 1*, rep 5 times. (25 sts)

Rnd 15: *Sc 3, dec 1*, rep 5 times. (20 sts)

Rnd 16: *Sc 2, dec 1*, rep 5 times. (15 sts)

Stuff lightly.

Rnd 17: *Sc 1, dec 1*, rep 5 times. (10 sts)

Rnd 18: Dec 5 times. (5 sts)

Fasten off.

Petals

Make 4 short and 7 long using pink yarn for all.

Rnd 1: Ch 2, 5 sc in second ch from hook.

Rnd 2: Sc 5.

Rnd 3: Sc 2 in each sc around. (10 sts)

Rnds 4–8: Sc 10.

For short petals: Fasten off, leaving long tail for sewing. Sew open end closed and sew petals next to each other on rnd 9 (where you worked into the back loops) of cushion.

For long petals:

Rnds 9 and 10: Sc 10.

Sl st 1 and fasten off, leaving long tail for sewing. Sew open end closed and sew long petals next to each other behind short petals on rnd 10 of cushion.

Little Tugboat

I had a little plastic tugboat when I was a young girl. It was great to play with in the water but it had no hugging potential. This crocheted one can't go in the water, but it's soft and plush . . . and huggable!

Finished Size

Approx 4½" high x 6" long

Materials

Worsted-weight yarn in brown, red, yellow, blue, and white
Size G-6 (4 mm) crochet hook
12 mm plastic eyes with safety backings
Black embroidery floss and embroidery needle
Tapestry needle
Fiberfill or stuffing of your choice

Hull

Start crocheting hull at bottom.
Using red yarn, ch 11.
Rnd 1: Sc 10 starting at second bump at back of ch (see "Working in Stitch Loops," page 171), ch 3, sc 10 on opposite side of ch (both loops of ch). (20 sc and 3 ch)
Rnd 2: Ch 3, *sc 10, sc 4 in ch-3 sp*, rep once on other side. (28 sts)
Rnd 3: *Sc 10, sc 2 in each of next 4 sts*, rep once on other side. (36 sts)
Rnd 4: *Sc 11, sc 2 in each of next 6 sts, sc 1*, rep once on other side. (48 sts)

Rnd 5: *Sc 13, sc 2 in next st, sc 6, sc 2 in next st, sc 3*, rep once on other side. (52 sts)
Rnd 6: *Sc 16, sc 2 in each of next 4 sts, sc 6*, rep once on other side. (60 sts)
Rnd 7: *Sc 19, sc 2 in each of next 2 sts, sc 9*, rep once on other side. (64 sts)
Rnd 8: *Sc 20, sc 2 in next 2 sts, sc 10*, rep once on other side. (68 sts)
Rnd 9: Sc 68 through back loops only.
Rnds 10–17: Sc 68.
Sl st 1 and fasten off.

Deck

Using brown yarn, work rnds 1–8 as for hull.
Rnd 9: Sc 68.
Sl st 1 and fasten off, leaving long tail for sewing. Position deck inside hull (approx ½" below edge of hull) sew three-quarters of the way around, stuff, and finish sewing.

Head

Rnd 1: Using blue yarn, ch 2, 5 sc in second ch from hook.
Rnd 2: Sc 2 in each sc around. (10 sts)
Rnd 3: *Sc 1, 2 sc in next sc*, rep 5 times. (15 sts)

Rnd 4: *Sc 2, 2 sc in next sc*, rep 5 times. (20 sts)
Rnd 5: *Sc 3, 2 sc in next sc*, rep 5 times. (25 sts)
Rnd 6: *Sc 4, 2 sc in next sc*, rep 5 times. (30 sts)
Rnd 7: *Sc 5, 2 sc in next sc*, rep 5 times. (35 sts)
Rnd 8: *Sc 6, 2 sc in next sc*, rep 5 times. (40 sts)
Rnd 9: Through back loops only, *sc 6, dec 1*, rep 5 times. (35 sts)
Rnds 10–15: Sc 35.
Sl st 1 and fasten off, leaving long tail for sewing.
Position and attach eyes. Embroider mouth. Stuff head and sew to deck.

Hat

Rnd 1: Using white yarn, ch 2, 5 sc in second ch from hook.

Rnd 2: Sc 2 in each sc around. (10 sts)

Rnd 3: *Sc 1, 2 sc in next sc*, rep 5 times. (15 sts)

Rnd 4: *Sc 2, 2 sc in next sc*, rep 5 times. (20 sts)

Rnds 5–7: Sc 20.

Rnd 8: Sc 20, turn.

Rnd 9: Through back loops only, *sc 3, 2 sc in next sc*, rep 5 times. Do not turn. (25 sts)

Rnds 10–12: Working in rnd again, sc 25.

Sl st 1 and fasten off. Stuff lightly and sew hat to head using white yarn.

Bumpers

Make 4.

Using yellow yarn, ch 15.

Rnd 1: Join first and last sts with sl st to form ring (being careful not to twist sts) and sc 15 inside the ring.

Rnds 2–6: Sc 15.

Sl st 1 and fasten off, leaving long tail for sewing. Fold piece and sew edges tog to form donut shape. Fasten off, leaving long tail for sewing. Sew 2 bumpers to each side of boat.

Mom and Baby Foxes

When Oli was in second grade she began reading a lot. Every couple of days she'd finish a big chapter book and was always asking for more. While she was reading *Fantastic Mr. Fox* by Roald Dahl, I thought it'd be nice to have some amigurumi foxes to go with the book.

Finished Sizes

Mom fox: Approx 5½" tall
Baby fox: Approx 4" tall

Materials

Worsted-weight yarn in orange, white, and blue
Size G-6 (4 mm) crochet hook
Plastic eyes with safety backings: 9 mm for baby and 12 mm for mom
Black embroidery floss and embroidery needle
Tapestry needle
Fiberfill or stuffing of your choice

Mom Fox

Muzzle

Rnd 1: Using orange yarn, ch 2, 6 sc in second ch from hook.
Rnd 2: Sc 2 in each sc around. (12 sts)
Rnds 3 and 4: Sc 12.
Rnd 5: *Sc 1, 2 sc in next sc*, rep 6 times. (18 sts)
Rnd 6: Sc 18.
Sl st 1 and fasten off, leaving long tail for sewing. Embroider nose and mouth and set aside.

Eye Roundies

Make 2.
Rnd 1: Using white yarn, ch 2, 6 sc in second ch from hook.
Rnd 2: Sc 2 in each sc around. (12 sts)
Rnd 3: *Sc 1, 2 sc in next sc*, rep 6 times. (18 sts)
Sl st 1 and fasten off, leaving long tail for sewing. Insert 12 mm eye through middle hole and set aside.

Head

Rnd 1: Using orange yarn, ch 2, 6 sc in second ch from hook.
Rnd 2: Sc 2 in each sc around. (12 sts)
Rnd 3: *Sc 1, 2 sc in next sc*, rep 6 times. (18 sts)
Rnd 4: *Sc 2, 2 sc in next sc*, rep 6 times. (24 sts)
Rnd 5: *Sc 3, 2 sc in next sc*, rep 6 times. (30 sts)
Rnd 6: *Sc 4, 2 sc in next sc*, rep 6 times. (36 sts)
Rnd 7: *Sc 5, 2 sc in next sc*, rep 6 times. (42 sts)
Rnds 8–17: Sc 42.
Rnd 18: *Sc 5, dec 1*, rep 6 times. (36 sts)
Rnd 19: *Sc 4, dec 1*, rep 6 times. (30 sts)
Stuff muzzle slightly and sew to face. Position and attach eyes (with eye roundies); sew eye roundies in place.
Rnd 20: *Sc 3, dec 1*, rep 6 times. (24 sts)
Rnd 21: *Sc 2, dec 1*, rep 6 times. (18 sts)
Stuff head.
Rnd 22: *Sc 1, dec 1*, rep 6 times. (12 sts)
Rnd 23: Dec 6 times. (6 sts)
Fasten off.

Ears

Make 2.
Rnd 1: Using orange yarn, ch 2, 5 sc in second ch from hook.
Rnd 2: Sc 5.
Rnd 3: Sc 2 in each sc around. (10 sts)
Rnds 4 and 5: Sc 10.
Rnd 6: *Sc 1, 2 sc in next sc*, rep 5 times. (15 sts)
Rnd 7: Sc 15.
Sl st 1 and fasten off, leaving long tail for sewing. Sew open end closed and sew ears to head.

Body

Rnd 1: Using orange yarn, ch 2, 6 sc in second ch from hook.

Rnd 2: Sc 2 in each sc around. (12 sts)

Rnd 3: *Sc 1, 2 sc in next sc*, rep 6 times. (18 sts)

Rnd 4: *Sc 2, 2 sc in next sc*, rep 6 times. (24 sts)

Rnd 5: *Sc 3, 2 sc in next sc*, rep 6 times. (30 sts)

Rnds 6–13: Sc 30.

Sl st 1 and fasten off, leaving long tail for sewing. Stuff and sew to head.

Arms and Legs

Make 4.

Rnd 1: Using orange yarn, ch 2, 5 sc in second ch from hook.

Rnd 2: Sc 2 in each sc around. (10 sts)

Rnds 3–8: Sc 10.

Sl st 1 and fasten off, leaving long tail for sewing. Stuff, sew open end of arms closed, and then sew arms and legs to body.

Tail

Rnd 1: Using white yarn, ch 2, 6 sc in second ch from hook.

Rnd 2: Sc 6.

Rnd 3: *Sc 1, 2 sc in next sc*, rep 3 times. (9 sts)

Rnd 4: Sc 9.

Rnd 5: *Sc 2, 2 sc in next sc*, rep 3 times. (12 sts)

Rnd 6: Sc 12.

Rnd 7: Using orange yarn, *sc 3, 2 sc in next sc*, rep 3 times. (15 sts)

Rnds 8–14: Sc 15.

Stuff almost to top.

Rnd 15: *Sc 3, dec 1*, rep 3 times. (12 sts)

Rnd 16: *Sc 2, dec 1*, rep 3 times. (9 sts)

Rnd 17: *Sc 1, dec 1*, rep 3 times. (6 sts)

Sl st 1 and fasten off, leaving long tail for sewing. Sew to body.

Little Scarf

Using blue yarn, loosely ch 72 and fasten off. Wrap around Mom's neck.

Baby Fox

Muzzle

Rnd 1: Using orange yarn, ch 2, 6 sc in second ch from hook.

Rnd 2: Sc 6.

Rnds 3–5: Sc 2 in each sc around. (12 sts)

Sl st 1 and fasten off, leaving long tail for sewing. Embroider nose and smile and set aside.

Eye Roundies

Make 2.

Rnd 1: Using white yarn, ch 2, 6 sc in second ch from hook.

Rnd 2: Sc 2 in each sc around. (12 sts)

Sl st 1 and fasten off, leaving long tail for sewing. Insert 9 mm eye through middle hole and set aside.

Head

Rnd 1: Using orange yarn, ch 2, 6 sc in second ch from hook.

Rnd 2: Sc 2 in each sc around. (12 sts)

Rnd 3: *Sc 1, 2 sc in next sc*, rep 6 times. (18 sts)

Rnd 4: *Sc 2, 2 sc in next sc*, rep 6 times. (24 sts)

Rnd 5: *Sc 3, 2 sc in next sc*, rep 6 times. (30 sts)

Rnds 6–13: Sc 30.

Stuff muzzle lightly and sew to face. Position and attach eyes (with eye roundies); sew eye roundies in place.

Body

Rnd 1: Using orange yarn, ch 2, 6 sc in second ch from hook.

Rnd 2: Sc 2 in each sc around. (12 sts)

Rnd 3: *Sc 1, 2 sc in next sc*, rep 6 times. (18 sts)

Rnds 4 and 5: Sc 18.

Rnds 6–8: Using blue yarn, sc 18.

Sl st 1 and fasten off, leaving long tail for sewing. Stuff and sew body to head.

Arms and Legs

Make 4.

Rnd 1: Using orange yarn, ch 2, 5 sc in second ch from hook.

Rnds 2–4: Sc 5.

Sl st 1 and fasten off, leaving long tail for sewing. Sew open end of arms closed, and then sew arms and legs to body.

Tail

Rnd 1: Using white yarn, ch 2, 6 sc in second ch from hook.

Rnd 2: Sc 6.

Rnd 3: *Sc 1, 2 sc in next sc*, rep 3 times. (9 sts)

Rnd 4: Change to orange yarn, sc 9.

Rnd 5: *Sc 2, 2 sc in next sc*, rep 3 times. (12 sts)

Rnds 6–8: Sc 12.

Stuff almost to top.

Rnd 9: Dec 6 times. (6 sts)

Sl st 1 and fasten off, leaving long tail to close 6-st hole. Sew tail to body.

Rnd 14: *Sc 3, dec 1*, rep 6 times. (24 sts)

Rnd 15: *Sc 2, dec 1*, rep 6 times. (18 sts)

Rnd 16: *Sc 1, dec 1*, rep 6 times. (12 sts)

Stuff head.

Rnd 17: Dec 6 times. (6 sts)

Fasten off.

Ears

Make 2.

Rnd 1: Using orange yarn, ch 2, 5 sc in second ch from hook.

Rnd 2: Sc 5.

Rnd 3: Sc 2 in each sc around. (10 sts)

Rnds 4–6: Sc 10.

Sl st 1 and fasten off, leaving long tail for sewing. Sew open end closed and sew ears to head.

Shy Little Unicorn

I showed my first attempt at making a unicorn to Oli and she said it was a cow! (She couldn't explain the horn.) Marti said my second attempt was a pig! So when I finished this one and they both said it was "a cute little unicorn," I knew I had finally finally succeeded. Make it brown and without the horn and have a pony, or maybe even add spots to make Oli's cow.

Finished Size

Approx 4½" tall x 6" long

Materials

Worsted-weight yarn in white and pink
Scraps of worsted-weight yarn in yellow, red, orange, green, purple, and blue
Size G-6 (4 mm) crochet hook
9 mm plastic eyes with safety backings
Small piece of pink craft felt
Tapestry needle
Fiberfill or stuffing of your choice

Head

Rnd 1: Using pink yarn, ch 2, 7 sc in second ch from hook.
Rnd 2: Sc 2 in each sc around. (14 sts)
Rnd 3: *Sc 1, 2 sc in next sc*, rep 7 times. (21 sts)
Rnd 4: *Sc 2, 2 sc in next sc*, rep 7 times. (28 sts)
Rnd 5: *Sc 3, 2 sc in next sc*, rep 7 times. (35 sts)
Rnds 6–9: Sc 35.

Rnd 10: Change to white yarn and sc 35.
Rnd 11: *Sc 3, dec 1*, rep 7 times. (28 sts)
Rnds 12 and 13: Sc 28.
Using pattern on page 167, cut 2 nostrils from pink felt and sew them to unicorn's nose.
Rnds 14–21: Sc 28.
Rnd 22: *Sc 2, dec 1*, rep 7 times. (21 sts)
Position and attach plastic eyes.
Rnd 23: *Sc 1, dec 1*, rep 7 times. (14 sts)
Stuff firmly.
Rnd 24: Dec 7 times. (7 sts)
Fasten off, leaving long tail to close 7-st hole.

Ears

Make 2.
Rnd 1: Using white yarn, ch 2, 4 sc in second ch from hook.
Rnd 2: Sc 2 in each sc around. (8 sts)
Rnds 3–7: Sc 8.
Sl st 1 and fasten off, leaving long tail for sewing. Sew ears to head.

Horn

Rnd 1: Using yellow yarn, ch 2, 4 sc in second ch from hook.
Rnd 2: Sc 4.
Rnd 3: *Sc 1, 2 sc in next sc*, rep one more time. (6 sts)
Rnds 4–8: Sc 6.
Sl st 1 and fasten off, leaving long tail for sewing. Sew horn to head.

Body

Rnd 1: Using white yarn, ch 2, 6 sc in second ch from hook.
Rnd 2: 2 sc in each sc around. (12 sts)
Rnd 3: *Sc 1, 2 sc in next sc*, rep 6 times. (18 sts)
Rnd 4: *Sc 2, 2 sc in next sc*, rep 6 times. (24 sts)
Rnds 5–10: Sc 24.
Rnd 11: *Sc 2, dec 1*, rep 6 times. (18 sts)
Rnds 12–14: Sc 18.
Rnd 15: *Sc 1, dec 1*, rep 6 times. (12 sts)
Rnds 16 and 17: Sc 12.
Sl st 1 and fasten off, leaving long tail for sewing. Stuff and sew body to head.

Legs

Make 4.

Rnd 1: Using pink yarn, ch 2, 6 sc in second ch from hook.

Rnd 2: Sc 2 in each sc around. (12 sts)

Rnd 3: Sc 12.

Rnds 4–14: Using white yarn, sc 12. Stuff lightly.

Rnd 15: Dec 6 times. (6 sts)

Fasten off, leaving long tail for sewing. Stuff slightly, sew open end closed, and sew legs to body.

Mane

This takes a while, but it makes the unicorn look so cute. Make 6 red, 6 orange, 6 green, 6 purple, and 6 blue.

Ch 12 and fasten off, leaving long tail for sewing. Sew to head, creating a part down the middle of the mane.

Tail

Make 4 using pink yarn.

Ch 24 and fasten off, leaving long tail for sewing. Sew tail to body.

Unicorn nostril

General Guidelines

Simple crochet skills are all you need to make these delightful amigurumi.

Yarn

The toys in this book are crocheted using worsted-weight yarn and a size G-6 (4 mm) crochet hook, and occasionally a size F-5 (3.75 mm) or E-4 (3.5 mm) hook. The yarn brands I used for the samples in this book is listed on page 174, but it doesn't really matter which brand you use.

Making amigurumi is a great way to use up leftover yarn. Choose colors similar to mine, or be creative and come up with your own color combinations! People often ask how many toys you can make from one 100-gram skein of worsted-weight yarn. While it varies, depending on the pattern and how tightly you crochet, I can usually make two to three of the larger animals and many, many small toys from just one 100-gram skein of main color. Of course you'll need other colors for some body parts and embellishments.

Gauge, Tension, and Hook Sizes

The measurements given for each toy are approximate and based on the way I crochet. I crochet pretty tightly, and my gauge is as follows:

4 sts and 5 rows = 1" with G hook and worsted-weight yarn

5 sts and 6 rows = 1" with F hook and worsted-weight yarn

The finished toy size, however, isn't really that important, so don't worry if your gauge is different from mine. Depending on your tension and the yarn you use, your toys might end up being a little bit smaller or larger than the ones I made. Changing to a bigger or smaller hook will give you a bigger or smaller toy, respectively.

Stitches

Simple stitches are used for these amigurumi projects, making them perfect for beginners.

Chain (ch). Make a slipknot and place it on the hook. Yarn over the hook, draw the yarn through the slipknot, and let the slipknot slide off the hook. *Yarn

over the hook, draw the yarn through the new loop, and let the loop slide off the hook. Repeat from * for the desired number of chains.

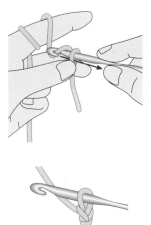

Slip stitch (sl st). A slip stitch is used to move across one or more stitches. Insert the hook into the stitch, yarn over the hook, and pull through both stitches at once.

Single crochet (sc). *Insert the hook into the chain or stitch indicated, yarn over the hook, and pull through the chain or stitch (two loops remain on the hook).

Yarn over the hook and pull through the remaining two loops on the hook. Repeat from * for the required number of stitches.

Back-post single crochet (BPsc). Insert the hook from the back around the vertical section, or post, of the single crochet stitch in the previous row and complete the single crochet stitch as usual. Repeat as directed to make a nice, slightly raised, braid-like row of stitches.

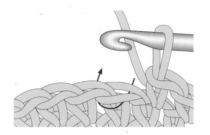

Single crochet increase. Work two single crochet stitches into the same stitch.

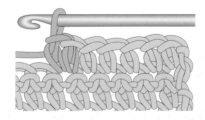

Single crochet decrease (dec). (Insert the hook into the next stitch, yarn over, pull up a loop) twice; yarn over and pull through all three loops on the hook.

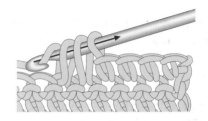

Half double crochet (hdc). *Yarn over the hook and insert the hook into the chain or stitch indicated. Yarn over the hook and pull through the stitch (three loops remain on the hook).

Yarn over the hook and pull through all three loops on the hook. Repeat from * for the required number of stitches.

Double crochet (dc). *Yarn over the hook and insert the hook into the chain or stitch indicated. Yarn over the hook and pull through the stitch (three loops are on the hook); yarn over the hook and pull through two loops on the hook (two loops remain on the hook).

Yarn over the hook and pull through the remaining two loops on the hook (one loop remains on the hook). Repeat from * for the required number of stitches.

Triple crochet (tr). *Yarn over the hook twice, insert the hook into the chain or stitch indicated. Yarn over the hook and pull through the stitch (four loops on the hook); yarn over the hook and pull through two loops on the hook (three loops remain on the hook).

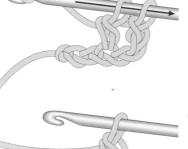

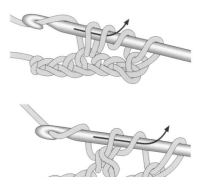

(Yarn over the hook and pull through two loops on the hook) twice (one loop remains on the hook). Repeat from * for the required number of stitches.

Working in Chain Loops

When crocheting the first row into the beginning chain, the first row of stitches is generally worked into one or both loops on the right side of the chain.

Crocheting into top loop

Crocheting into both loops

For some projects, the first row of stitches is worked in the "bump" on the wrong side of the chain.

Crocheting into the bump

Working in Stitch Loops

The majority of the stitches are worked in both loops of the stitches from the previous row. There are a few projects where you will work a row into the back loop or the front loop of the stitch.

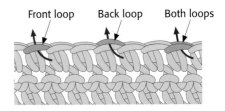

Front loop   Back loop   Both loops

Crocheting in the Round

When crocheting in the round, you'll crochet around and around, forming a continuous spiral. To keep track of where the rounds begin and end, mark the end or beginning of a round with a safety pin, stitch marker, or little piece of yarn pulled through one of the stitches. At the end of the last round, slip-stitch in the first single crochet of the previous round and fasten the yarn off.

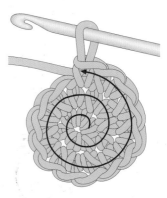

Changing Yarn Colors

Some projects require alternating two colors in the body. To do this, work the last stitch of a round until one step remains in the stitch; then work the last step with the new color and continue the round in the new color. Continue to the end of the round and change color in the same manner.

Adding Faces

Although I've used plastic eyes with safety backings on all of the toys, you can instead embroider the eyes, use buttons, or cut out and sew on little pieces of felt. For each pattern, eye sizes are given in millimeters.

The templates for the muzzles and any other pieces to be cut from felt are included with each project. Cut the felt pieces with sharp scissors to get nice, smooth edges. Using embroidery floss and a needle, I use simple stitches to "draw" the faces on the felt before attaching the felt pieces to the project. Sew on pieces of felt with a sharp needle and matching sewing thread. Use a very small running stitch close to the edge of the piece.

Safety

Plastic eyes with safety backings are nearly impossible to take out—I've tried! I would not, however, give a toy with plastic eyes (or buttons) to children younger than three years old unless they are being supervised at all times while playing with them. Eyes cut from craft felt or embroidered eyes are a better choice for young children.

Mouths. For a simple mouth, bring the needle out at point A and insert the needle at point B, leaving a loose strand of yarn to form the mouth. Once you're happy with the shape of the mouth, bring the needle out again at point C, cross over the loose strand of yarn, and insert the needle at point D to make a tiny stitch. Secure the yarn ends on the wrong side.

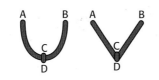

Satin stitch noses and eyes. Bring the needle out through point A, insert at point B, and repeat, following the shape you want for the nose or eyes and making sure to work the stitches really close together. Secure the ends on the wrong side.

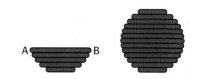

Another option for embroidering a nose is to work from a center point upward. Bring the needle up from underneath at point A; insert the needle at point B. Bring the needle up at point C, very close to point A. Insert the needle back into point B. Continue working stitches close to each other to create a triangle, making sure to always insert the needle back into point B. When you're satisfied with the triangle, make two long stitches across the top of the nose to help define it.

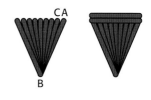

Stuffing

Stuff your toys firmly so they retain their shape and don't look "droopy." Be careful not to overstuff them, though, because the stuffing will stretch the fabric and may show through the stitches.

I always use polyester fiberfill stuffing because it's nonallergenic, won't bunch up, and it's washable, which is always good when you're making toys! If you do wash the toys, make sure you follow the yarn care instructions on the label.

Adding the Extremities

Use a tapestry needle and the same color of yarn as the pieces (or at least one of the pieces) that you want to sew together. When sewing pieces to the body, make sure they are securely attached so that little fingers can't pull them off.

On some animals, the opening of the extremities will remain open for sewing onto the body; the instructions will tell you when to leave them open. Position the limb on the body and sew all around it, going through the front stitches of both the limb and the body.

On other animals, the opening of the extremities will be sewn closed before being attached to the body. To do this, pinch the opening closed, line up the stitches of one side with the other side, and sew through the front loop of one side and the back loop of the other side. Position the piece where you want it on the body and sew.

Weaving in Ends

Weaving in ends is easy on little amigurumi pieces. Because the pieces are stuffed, simply pull the thread tails to the inside of the piece and leave them. The tails will be secure inside the pieces. If there are any yarn tails left after sewing the pieces together, insert the needle into the body, pull it out 1" or 2" away, and snip close to the piece, being careful not to cut the crochet stitches.

Abbreviations and Glossary

*	repeat directions between * and * as many times as indicated	rnd(s)	round(s)
		RS	right side
		sc	single crochet
BPsc	back-post single crochet	sk	skip
ch	chain	sl st	slip stitch
dc	double crochet	sp	space
dec	decrease (see "Single Crochet Decrease" on page 169)	st(s)	stitch(es)
		tog	together
hdc	half double crochet	tr	triple crochet
rem	remaining	WS	wrong side
rep	repeat		

Resources

Yarn

Caron
www.Caron.com

Lion Brand Yarn
www.LionBrand.com

Patons
www.PatonsYarns.com

Red Heart
www.CoatsandClark.com

Safety Eyes

Your local craft store probably carries safety eyes. If you can't find them locally, visit www.SunshineCrafts.com; search for "eyes." They ship them fast. If you want fun, colorful eyes, check out www.SuncatcherEyes.net.

About the Author

Ana Paula Rímoli of Bloomfield, New Jersey, was born in Montevideo, Uruguay, and learned to crochet as a child. She began crocheting toys when her own children were born and now hosts her own popular blog featuring her crocheted designs. Visit Ana's blog or her online Etsy store:

AmigurumiPatterns.blogspot.com

Etsy.com/shop/AnaPaulaOli

What's your creative passion?

Find it at **ShopMartingale.com**

books • eBooks • ePatterns • daily blog • free projects
videos • tutorials • inspiration • giveaways

Martingale®
Create with Confidence

You might also enjoy these fine titles.